# Enactments

EDITED BY

RICHARD SCHECHNER

To perform is to imagine, represent, live and enact present circumstances, past events and future possibilities. Performance takes place across a very broad range of venues from city streets to the countryside, in theatres and in offices, on battlefields and in hospital operating rooms. The genres of performance are many, from the arts to the myriad performances of everyday life, from courtrooms to legislative chambers, from theatres to wars to circuses.

ENACTMENTS encompasses performance in as many of its aspects and realities as there are authors able to write about them.

ENACTMENTS includes active scholarship, readable thought and engaged analysis across the broad spectrum of performance studies.

## Praise for *Source Work for Actors*

'Much like Toporkov's *Stanislavski in Rehearsal*, we accompany Diane as she throws herself wholeheartedly into the unknown, facing the physical and psychological challenges of a variety of acting exercises, and courageously stepping into the whirlwind of creation. Her compelling memoir details Cynkutis' impeccable ability to synthesize and pass on his many years of work with Grotowski. Her confrontations with the concepts of association, rhythm, group improvisation, and work on one's self are meaningful lessons for all of us working in the theatre. But the real revelation of the book is Diane herself. She put me back in the studio stalking those elusive moments of creativity.'

—**James Slowiak**, Co-artistic Director, New World Performance Laboratory; Professor Emeritus of Theatre, The University of Akron; Co-author, *Jerzy Grotowski*

'Diane Edgecomb has written a remarkable book. She invites the reader to join her personal odyssey through the rigors of an intensive theater workshop led by one of Jerzy Grotowski's leading actors, Zbigniew Cynkutis, in 1984.Through the specific challenges, difficulties, exhaustion and personal breakthroughs that she undergoes, she allows us to both get lost with her and then to be found again. Part documentary and part memoir, the journey is both instructive and fully engaging.'

—**Anne Bogart**, Theatre and Opera Director

'This book gets inside the rigorous work of surrender that is the essence of any artist's work. It's about falling in love with a practice in the very specific wonderful moment that was the blossoming of training and art that came out of the "Poor Theatre". It will be familiar, comforting and inspiring to students and teachers alike who grapple with the questions how do we become deeper, wilder, and more porous as humans and as artists.'

—**Deirdre O'Connell**, Actor of Stage and Film; 2022 Tony Award Winner

# Source Work for Actors

## In Workshop with Zbigniew Cynkutis of Grotowski's Laboratory Theatre

DIANE EDGECOMB

LONDON NEW YORK CALCUTTA

**Seagull Books, 2025**

First published in volume form by Seagull Books, 2025



Cover photograph: Diane Edgecomb in *Restraints* (2012).
Photograph by Melina Giorgi, courtesy of the author.

Cover design: Sunandini Banerjee, Seagull Books.

Hardcover ISBN 978 1 80309 516 5

Paperback ISBN 978 1 80309 517 2

**British Library Cataloguing-in-Publication Data**
A catalogue record for this book is available from the British Library

Typeset by Seagull Books, Calcutta, India
Printed and bound in the USA by Integrated Books International

*This book is dedicated to*
*Zbigniew Cynkutis (1938–1987)*
*Actor, Director, and Beloved Teacher*

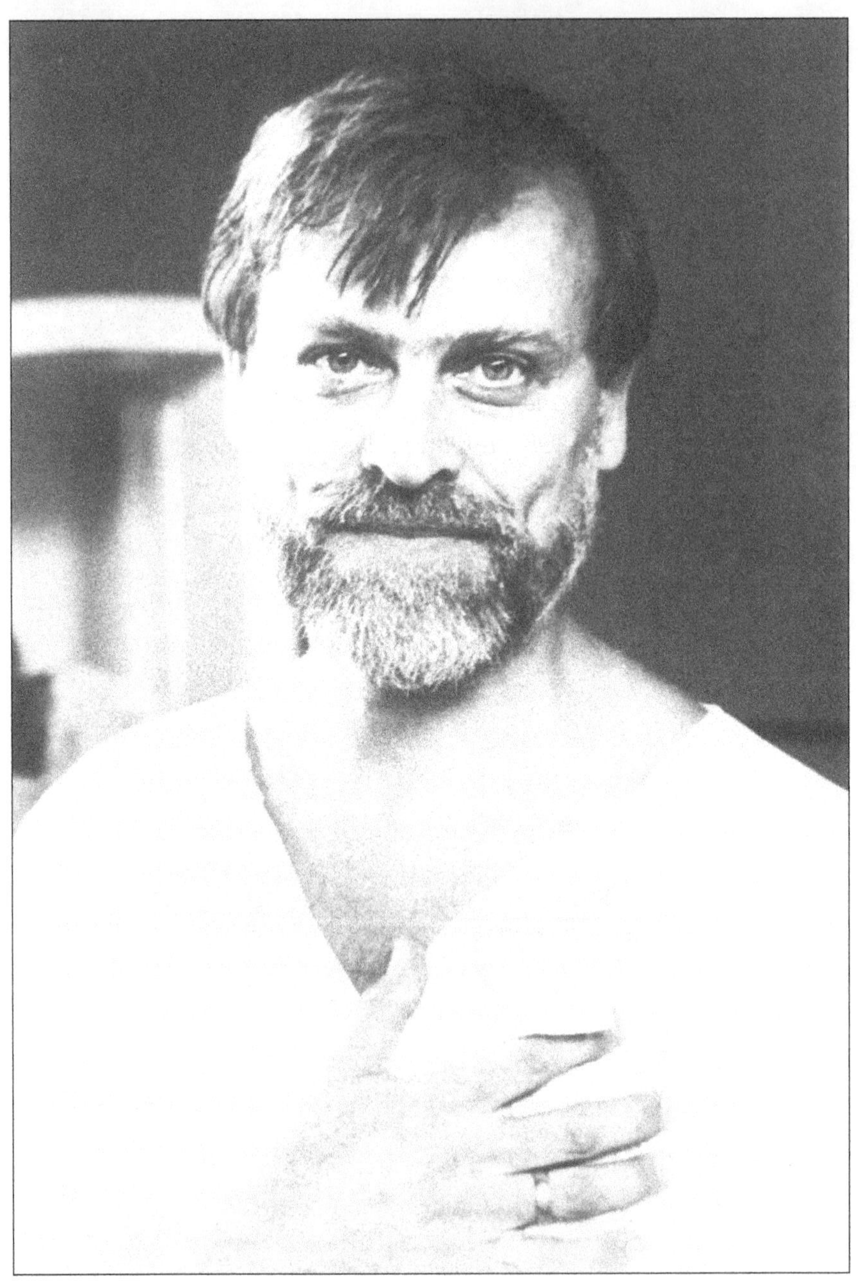

**FIGURE 1.** Zbigniew Cynkutis
*Photograph by Marek Grotowski. Courtesy of Richard Mennen.*

*The idea of theatre at the beginning was not to show people something like stories, but to provide people with food for their spirit, food for feelings, food for this life which we have inside of us.*

—Zbigniew Cynkutis, June 1984

## CONTENTS

# FOREWORD

Jenna Kumiega

More than half a century ago, I stepped into an unfamiliar performance space in Poland, clutching a precious ticket for a theatrical event that would become an iconic masterpiece: Jerzy Grotowski's *Apocalypsis Cum Figuris*. The room was full of shadows and the air was rich with muted, rustling expectation. The experience that followed changed the direction of my life.

Intellectually I understood little of what was said or done: not the resonant Polish voices that seemed to shake the rough brick walls and echo in the cavern of my chest, nor the dramatic physical interactions between the extraordinary actors, who appeared to fly through space.

At one moment, an actor landed in a crouch, inches from where I sat cross-legged on the floor: feeling my sense of shock, she reached out a hand to cradle my ankle momentarily. Another actor, his body fluid with coiled intention, intoned a lengthy speech directly to me. Our eyes locked together as I felt the energy of his words rise in me. My body was electrified, and only when he turned away did I remember to breathe. The actor was Zbigniew Cynkutis.

I returned to the Apocalypsis space countless times before the final performance of *Apocalypsis Cum Figuris* in May 1980, and worked on many occasions with the Laboratory Theatre, mostly during the paratheatrical phase of work between 1975 and 1981. My active research, which also included taped interviews with Cynkutis and most of the other actors, led in turn to a book—*The Theatre of Grotowski* (1985).

Through this six-year process of research, I came to understand better the central factor that had first drawn me to Grotowski and his actors. These performers proposed and embodied a new and different relationship with those who came to witness their work. There was a dynamic, energetic connection between us, created by the intensity of their presence and channelled by the extraordinary rigour and power of their practice. This was what my body recognised during that first overwhelming experience in 1972.

When I read the initial draft of Diane Edgecomb's documentation of the workshop she experienced with Cynkutis, I found myself transported back to all the spaces in which I had either worked with the Laboratory Theatre or watched their performances. I could still see the gleam of the floors, buffed by the bare feet of so many participants eager to explore further the energetic presence of those skilled actors and workshop leaders. Most of all I could still feel the dynamic intensity of the spaces, full of possibility.

I may have met Diane Edgecomb during the conference hosted by Kent University in the UK as part of the 2009 UNESCO Year of Grotowski, although neither of us can remember definitively. We had both previously shared a warm and close friendship with Zbyszek and Jola Cynkutis. So many years after Zbyszek's death, Diane had travelled with Jola and Jola's partner Khalid Tyabji from Poland to Canterbury for the conference. Jola and Khalid were always keen to bring mutual friends together, so they probably introduced us.

Ten years later, Diane made contact with me again, explaining that she was working on a book documenting an intensive workshop with Cynkutis that took place in the US in 1984. She wondered whether I might consider taking a look at her text. That was the start of more than four years of correspondence that segued from 'having a look' at her book to an intimate engagement with many aspects of her committed journey—bringing Zbigniew Cynkutis and his unique qualities to life for a new generation of seekers.

I am more than happy to have been peripherally involved in Diane's project, because of the unique value of her ethnographic approach to performance research and documentation, which was not common practice during the time of Grotowski's *Teatr Laboratorium*. Neither Grotowski himself nor the original actor-members of his company are still living. And the number of those who worked directly with them—and therefore had the benefit of experiencing the embodied and technical processes in an unadulterated form—will continue to dwindle.

These factors mean that new first-person narratives of the kind that Diane Edgecomb offers have both poignancy and added value. She has skilfully woven together documentation of the workshop events with painstaking transcriptions of Cynkutis' own words, enlivened by extracts of her journals from that time. An additional gift accompanying her book is a link to extracts of the original audio tapes made during the workshop. Despite the acoustic limitations of remastered cassettes, the mesmerizing power of Cynkutis' voice still takes me back to my first witnessing of *Apocalypsis* in 1972.

The fact that Diane has been able to achieve all this from a perspective of forty years speaks of her dedication to honouring the legacy of one of Grotowski's most charismatic actors.

Diane's book also offers something of equal importance—readability. She has an open and authentic way of tracking her own process throughout the workshop and recording her subjective experiences. She is unafraid to expose her uncertainties or preconceptions, especially in her journal entries. In this way she is an enjoyable and accessible writer, not only for those already familiar with Grotowski but also for students or general readers who may not be experienced in this form of creative work.

Through detailed and precise documenting of the exercises, Diane gradually builds a record of the kind of training that would have taken place in Laboratory Theatre spaces. Some of the exercises and directions would have originated from Grotowski, developed by himself, or sourced from performance masters in other cultures throughout his years of training and research. Some of them would have been developed by the actors themselves, encouraged by Grotowski to explore their unique strengths and disseminate their own training, and this is the path that Cynkutis took.

Equally valuable is the commentary on the atmosphere and attitude Cynkutis was requiring of the participants, a kind of dedication and ethos decidedly unfamiliar at that time to acting students in the West. Diane calls this 'sacred space' and 'an invitation to deeper parts of ourselves to be present'.

All these aspects of the workshop are channelled through Diane's authentic and grounded commentary on her own internal process. She charts the struggles—so familiar to beginners in this field of work—between intellect and instinct, reality and delusion, body and mind.

While respecting the mystery of some aspects of training and practice, she never intentionally mystifies. Instead, she seeks to describe the experiences and effects through her own body—and through what she witnesses in the bodies of Cynkutis and the other participants. That focus brings the account of the workshop to life and carries something of the power of the original experience.

Ultimately, it seems to me that this book is a gift from the past to the present, and to the future. It brings to mind a quote from Kermit Dunkelberg, one of the actors of Cynkutis' international company in Wrocław in 1986–87: 'My writing can never replace, much less erase, the experience of those who were "there". It is, rather, for those who were "not there": for those who come after and seek a trace.'

*January 2025*

# PREFACE

In June 1984, the US-based director and professor of theatre Richard Mennen received a spirited phone call from his friend, Zbigniew Cynkutis. A leading member of the famed Polish Laboratory Theatre, Cynkutis was a master actor and accomplished director. He had just finished several years as a visiting professor of theatre at Hamilton College, Clinton, New York, where he focused on advancing theatre training for actors. In the phone call, Cynkutis described to Mennen the remarkable progress he was making with a small group of actors and university students in his summer workshop intensive at Hamilton College. In a short but condensed period, the group was achieving results he had been striving for over many years and he wanted Mennen to know.

This positive leap forward in training practices was especially important to Cynkutis because, at that time, his future was uncertain. His position as a visiting professor was coming to an end without an offer of any permanent appointment. Back in his homeland of Poland, the political situation was unstable and living conditions grim after several years under martial law.[1] To add to the uncertainty, Cynkutis had just received the startling news that, without consulting him, the other members of the Laboratory Theatre had decided to dissolve the company. The director of the theatre, Jerzy Grotowski, had already left Poland to seek political asylum in the United States.

1 In December 1981, Poland—then a satellite state of the USSR—was placed under martial law in reaction to pro-democracy movements. The resulting restrictions, which stayed in effect until July 1983, put additional stress on an already weakened economy: 'There was a curfew; intensified food rationing; theatres and cinemas were closed; and people were forbidden to gather in large groups or leave town without permission' (Kumiega 1985: 212).

The 10-day intensive Cynkutis was leading at Hamilton College was to be his last workshop in the US before returning home to begin anew. Perhaps that's why, during the workshop, he took the creative risks that he did. Working with a small, chosen number of participants, Cynkutis introduced a method of animating group energies—a technique known not only to Cynkutis but to other core Laboratory Theatre members. Until that moment, this method had never been openly discussed, documented, or shared. The resulting developments in the work were startling and full of possibility.

I was one of the five students in that workshop at Hamilton College. Despite the passage of time, I feel compelled to write this account both to document Cynkutis' teaching methods and to tell the story of my encounter with this influential actor. This book offers a rare window into the training practices of a consummate theatre artist, one of Grotowski's leading actors and one of his major collaborators.

My own work has been continually enriched and informed by the valuable training I received from Cynkutis. Among the lines of exploration that proved foundational to me are the following: how to draw from elements of nature as a direct source for theatre work; the importance of grounding the actor's dynamic expression in opposing vectors; how to activate a role by finding deep, organic associations; how to access the conjuring power that occurs when Body–Voice–Image are linked; and how the voice alone can create not only *transferable emotional experiences* but the *reality of an image in the space*. These last possibilities were clearly demonstrated to us by the transformative power of Cynkutis' voice.

All of Cynkutis' training exercises were accompanied by his insight into the vital importance of having the right approach to a task. He showed us that investing our whole selves, with both rigour and honesty, was as important as the task itself. He also clearly demonstrated the dedication one needs to pursue a path in theatre in line with one's highest ideals.

For many years, I've been working to reconstruct the workshop, drawing from the extensive notes I took during session breaks and my impressions written at the end of each day. I've contacted fellow students to tap their recollections and, because the workshop was recorded, I've spent countless hours transcribing audio recordings of Cynkutis' instructions, comments, and conversations.

Cynkutis' use of language, the intentionality of his speech and the timing of his pauses, was critical to his communication. For this reason, and so that others can hear instructions and reflections given in his own voice, I've made many of the audio recordings available online. At certain key points throughout the text, I've indicated where there are accompanying recordings. Even though the audio is compromised by its age and by the variety of spaces we were in, Cynkutis' presence and unmistakable voice are captured forever, preserved in this unique moment in time. The QR code at the end of this preface gives access to a playlist of all the numbered recordings. Several additional audio files of interest are included as well.

For this book, I've lightly edited the transcripts so that they read with more brevity and ease. Cynkutis was not completely fluent in English, and I've corrected some usage, while still keeping the idiosyncrasies and dynamics of his language as well as his carefully chosen wording intact.

Workshops led by Laboratory Theatre actors were intense. They engaged the deepest layers of the psyche and called on participants to push themselves well beyond their normal limits. There are elements in this way of working that may seem alien to theatre practitioners today. I invite the reader to remain open to the search we were on, to the deep commitment required, and to the full range of bodily expression that is at the heart of the Laboratory Theatre's work.

This was no ordinary workshop. During the time we were in his company, Cynkutis took the five of us on a profound journey. He drew upon methods derived and adapted from his years working closely with

Grotowski as well as from his own evolving research into the actor's craft. Cynkutis was on a mission uniquely his: to articulate and pass on an approach to working with dramatic scripts grounded in the processes of the Laboratory Theatre. In our workshop, he used this approach to help us explore characterization as well as scenes and monologues from traditional plays, in this case, Eugene O'Neill's *Long Day's Journey into Night* (1956).

The performances Grotowski directed were known for their uncompromising rigour, challenging physicality, sheer visceral power, and psychic depth. His experimental productions were not presentations of dramatic texts as such, but a deep response to classic plays and a confrontation with the societal questions they raised. This response was articulated through carefully crafted and dynamic montages of text, immersive scenic elements, and, most importantly, the presence and expressive life of the actors themselves. His skilful directorial work and the legendary abilities of his actors earned him and his company international recognition and fame. However, unlike some other great theatrical innovators, such as Konstantin Stanislavsky and Michael Chekhov, Grotowski was not interested in creating a transferable technique or theatre method, insisting instead that his successors develop their own approaches to the work. In characteristically enigmatic terms, Grotowski stated his attitude to the notion of theatrical method: 'When I came to the conclusion that the problem of building my own system was illusory and that there exists no ideal system which could be a key to creativity, then the word "method" changed its meaning for me. There exists a challenge, to which *each must give his own answer*' (in Kumiega 1985: 111; my emphasis).[2]

*Towards a Poor Theatre* (1968) outlined the training Grotowski and his group developed as well as some of their guiding principles and was

---

2 For a detailed discussion of Grotowski's reasoning for not codifying a method for his theatre work, see *The Theatre of Grotowski* (Kumiega 1985: 45–46, 109–26).

a major influence in the spread of this visceral form of theatre from the late 1960s onwards. But neither the book nor Grotowski's subsequent essays constitute a guide to acting technique. Most of the day-to-day working practices of the Laboratory Theatre elaborated during their Theatre of Productions phase were never recorded and remained in the hands of his close circle of colleagues, most of whom are now deceased. Given the dearth of documentation, this book is a valuable resource detailing Cynkutis' active search for the best way to impart his knowledge. Cynkutis was uniquely positioned to interpret and pass on this work to other seekers. Not only was he involved at the deepest level in the development of the acting and training processes of the Laboratory Theatre, he also worked extensively in more traditional theatre venues and, in later years, embarked on his own course of study and vocation as a director.

During our intensive, Cynkutis' openness when speaking about process was both refreshing and insightful. His dedication to theatre as an art form was unwavering and deep. Considered by many to be the intellectual of the company,[3] Cynkutis often strove to return the Laboratory Theatre to its earlier theatre production-oriented phase. He humorously called himself 'conservative' and, as Grotowski's search led him to ever more participatory and exploratory models, Cynkutis believed that his own emphasis on making theatre pieces created an important second vector, countering Grotowski's movement towards the esoteric.[4] Cynkutis was looking for ways to pass on the work process in an accessible and objective form while still keeping its rigour, honesty, commitment, and

---

3 As Jola Cynkutis would later note: 'Cynkutis was probably unique amongst actors of the Laboratory Theatre in the fact that, apart from being a splendid actor, he was a thinker and a scholar who made extensive notes about everything he did and thought about. He was not merely a Grotowskian actor, a follower of the master, but somebody who maintained an independent perspective on the methods and work he was part of—always in dialogue' (in Karafistan 2003: 168).

4 Richard Mennen, a close friend and colleague of Cynkutis, shared these observations in an interview with me (Mennen 2022).

full-body engagement. His quest was to tether the Laboratory Theatre's remarkable discoveries to its original intent: a fully engaged theatre rooted in the psycho-physical processes of the actor.

Cynkutis' tragic death in an automobile accident on an icy road in Poland on 9 January 1987 at the age of only 48 deprived the world of a major theatrical innovator. It occurred only three years after our workshop, and just before I was able to act on his invitation to join the international company he was creating. He was in the process of establishing a strong theatrical model, exploring, developing, and transmitting his work through the 'second vector' he had created in Poland: The Second Studio based in the former seat of the Laboratory Theatre in Wrocław. I believe he used his workshop with us and with others in the US as a means of developing and formalizing his ideas and was putting them into practice.

Over my years as a theatre artist, I've been involved with numerous Grotowski-inspired theatre companies ranging from Stage One Theatre Lab in the late 1970s to Double Edge Theatre in the early '90s. I've taken many workshops with luminous teachers, including leading Laboratory Theatre actor Rena Mirecka. However, this encounter with Cynkutis, at a time when he was poised to return to his homeland to establish a new company, remains the most potent and influential learning experience of my life.

I'll let this story of my encounter with Cynkutis, or Zbyszek as he affectionately let us call him, unfold as I experienced it at the time and from my beginner's point of view, filled as it is with the vulnerability and idealism of a young seeker. I'll recount it by moving slowly, step-by-step, session-by-session through the workshop from its beginning with exercises that may be familiar to those who have studied Grotowski's practical work, through challenging approaches created by Cynkutis himself, to its unpredictable conclusion.

Along the way, the reader may glimpse the possibility of a new theatre animated and transformed by deep energetic sources and reinvigorated by the mysteries still to be discovered in the actor's craft. I hope you, the reader, will encounter new perspectives and fresh insights and gain some sense of the depth, wisdom, and charisma of the man himself.

*Diane Edgecomb*

*January 2025*

**FIGURE 2.** Zbigniew Cynkutis and Rena Mirecka
in *The Tragical History of Doctor Faustus* (1963).
*Photograph by Opiola-Moskwiak. Courtesy of Maria Cynkutis.*

INTRODUCTION

# ZBIGNIEW CYNKUTIS

Zbigniew Cynkutis[1] was in the midst of pursuing a successful career as an actor of stage and screen when, in 1961, in Opole, Poland, a local theatre director by the name of Jerzy Grotowski came to his door with a problem. An actor in Grotowski's Teatr 13 Rzędów (Theatre of Thirteen Rows)[2] playing the major role of Guślarz, the Sorcerer, in their upcoming production of *Dziady* (Forefathers' Eve, 1961) had got drunk and then completely disappeared just days before their premiere. Grotowski needed someone to take on the role but, if Cynkutis agreed, he would have to learn, rehearse, and perform the part in less than a week—an almost impossible task. Intrigued by the role and the difficult challenge, Cynkutis agreed. For the next several days he barely slept, learning the part in an unbelievably short amount of time—saving the premiere.

During our Hamilton College workshop, Cynkutis referenced the company's reaction to what he had done with youthful delight: 'I think that they were very impressed with what I did. [ . . . ] They were more and more often, including Grotowski, asking me why I will not come forever' (Cynkutis 1984).

In a 1981 interview with Jenna Kumiega, Cynkutis spoke of his own deep response to working with the company:

---

1 A detailed biography is available at the official website of the Grotowski Institute based in Wrocław (Grotowski Institute 2012a). See also Paul Allain's beautifully written and comprehensive preface in Zbigniew Cynkutis' *Acting with Grotowski* (Allain 2015).

2 The name of the theatre in Opole, Poland, where Grotowski was director. He later renamed it Teatr Laboratorium (Laboratory Theatre).

> Although these people had been called dilettantes by those wiser than I, what I found there gave me hope. There was something I hadn't met in the conventional theatre or even during study—I mean the discipline of those on the stage. There was construction, structure, consciousness, and there was risk. It was something they did with belief, trust and with hope [ . . . ]. I felt that this group had respect for those coming to see them, even when it was such a small number. There was something between them and each visitor. (in Kumiega 1985: 13–14)

Cynkutis joined the company and went on to play the leading role in such productions as *Kordian* (1962) and *The Tragical History of Doctor Faustus* (1963).[3] During the rehearsal process for *Faustus*, Cynkutis' collaboration with Grotowski was intense, involving many months of extensive one-on-one sessions. His resulting performance as Faustus was seminal, breaking new ground both in the method that Grotowski used and in its implications for the actor. Cynkutis' own meticulous notebooks describe the process he undertook when training for and performing the role. Within his candid and startling account (Cynkutis 2015a: 154–64) one can see the considerable demands made on every aspect of the actor's personhood: body, mind, emotional life, and soul to reach what Grotowski called the 'total act'.[4]

Although the production never toured outside Poland, *Faustus* became an international sensation when participants attending the

---

3 A short video excerpt of Cynkutis in the title role of Faustus can be found at Grotowski Institute (2012b).

4 'This act can be attained only out of the experience of one's own life, this act which strips, bares, unveils, reveals, and uncovers. Here an actor should not act but rather penetrate the regions of his own experience with his body and voice . . . [ . . . ] this is neither a story nor the creation of an illusion; it is the present moment. The actor exposes himself and . . . he discovers himself. Yet he has to know how to do this anew each time' (Grotowski, quoted in the Polish theatre journal *Dialog* [1969], cited in Osiński 1986: 85–86).

Tenth Congress of the International Theatre Institute, held in Warsaw in 1963, were taken to see it in the city of Łódź. Eugenio Barba, who was Grotowski's assistant for *Faustus,* arranged for a busload of international delegates to travel the 140 km from Warsaw to Łódź. 'After its premiere, [*The*] *Tragical History of Doctor Faustus* inspired about one hundred reviews, essays and studies in the West' (Osiński 1986: 76). The success of the performance firmly laid the groundwork for the company's reputation abroad.

In her article on theatre work and shamanic practice, Rachel Karafistan compares Cynkutis' intensive preparation for every performance of *Faustus* to the preparation required for a shamanic journey, drawing attention to the inner, mystical waters Cynkutis was navigating:

> In this rare, humble, and beautiful insight into the preparation, work, and experience of one actor, it is possible to intuit and identify many shamanic dimensions. For example, the total awakening of the senses in order to reach a state akin to the feeling of being 'sucked into the interior'; the disorientation of the actor on returning to consciousness; the necessity to have faith and to go so far as to locate that universal point which is 'hidden in everyone, identical feelings, reactions and thoughts'; the likening of reaching a suitable and open physical state in which one may feel that s/he can 'fly'; and finally the pre-performance meditative process which, as here described, bears more than a passing resemblance to the trance-inducing procedures of the shamans of old. (Karafistan 2003: 164–65)

This was a developing process within the Laboratory Theatre and, though similar to other trance states, Grotowski's investigations were also unique. In his article 'The Empty Room: Studying Jerzy Grotowski's *Towards a Poor Theatre*', Franco Ruffini describes in great detail the care with which Grotowski sought to define an actor's pathway to 'trance':[5]

---

5 Ruffini provides an illuminating backstory on Grotowski's attempts to define what he was finding in his work with the actor. Ultimately, Ruffini posits that it was more

> Only by going beyond all this [physical technique] does it become possible to achieve trance, and the actor can liberate that living stream of impulses which is the 'process'. And going 'beyond all this' not only means going beyond Stanislavsky, but also beyond representational performance. [ . . . ] The organicity that flows in the 'process' is a 'further' organicity [beyond daily life] in which body-heart-head rediscover an original unity on a higher level. (2009: 109)

Years earlier, Grotowski himself said this about trance: 'The actor makes a total gift of himself. This is a technique of the 'trance' and of the integration of all the actor's psychic and bodily powers which emerge from the most intimate layers of his being and his instinct, springing forth in a sort of "translumination"' (1968: 16).

This was not just *acting*; this theatre practice had spiritual dimensions.[6] What emerged through this research was a process that went well beyond ordinary experience, a genuinely altered state which, similar to trance-like and ecstatic states in other spiritual traditions, had energetic dimensions. However, in order to be replicated within a theatrical model, the actor's journey needed to be repeatable and linked to a 'score'[7] of actions and impulses. This score created a riverbed for the current, for the unfolding process. It was not until Grotowski was developing the performance *The Constant Prince* (1965) with actor Ryszard Cieślak that

---

important to Grotowski to leave the definition open or, as Ruffini metaphorically states, to leave this room 'empty' rather than to define the approach too narrowly (2009: 93–111).

6 For a scholarly exploration of the influences on Grotowski's research from a variety of spiritual traditions, see *Rethinking Religion in the Theatre of Grotowski* by Catharine Christoff. In her own words, the study 'maps the specific dynamics of the relation between the body and the spiritual in Grotowski's work [ . . . ]' (2017: vii).

7 Grotowski did not so much focus on the terms 'character' and 'role' in his theatrical productions but instead used the musical term 'score' to refer to the precise and repeatable elements of the actor's journey through the performance.

he was able to have the 'process' happen on a consistent basis in front of an audience.[8]

It was in 1963, sometime after the opening of Faustus, that Cynkutis had what he termed a 'crisis' in the work (Cynkutis 1984). Later that year, he made the difficult decision to leave the Laboratory Theatre to perform with other, more conventional, Polish companies in theatre and film. From September 1963 through most of 1966, Cynkutis did not take part in the theatre's rehearsal process for new work although he continued to appear in earlier performances such as *Akropolis* and *Faustus.*

For Cynkutis, there may have been many factors that led to his leave-taking. The financial situation of the theatre, difficult as always, was becoming ever more uncertain. Even the question of whether the actors would be receiving their next month's salary was sometimes unclear. Cynkutis and his wife Maria (née Gregorek) had just had their first child, Magdalena, in January 1963 and it would have been difficult to balance the needs of a new family with the financial insecurity and overwhelming demands of the theatre.

But there were other reasons for the split. Cynkutis found that he was physically and psychologically exhausted from the work on *Faustus.* As noted by the Grotowski Institute: 'This was highly intimate work which penetrated extremely deep into the actor's most intimate experiences' (Grotowski.net 2012a). The structure of the role was built on deeply personal memories chosen for their potentially explosive, cathartic energetic charge. And, despite the 'extraordinary respect [ . . . ] and something like love' (Cynkutis 2015b: 76) that Grotowski gave to Cynkutis as he explored

8 'In working on the role of Faustus, particularly his final monologue, Grotowski together with Zbigniew Cynkutis attempted for the very first time to bring about the total act. This was only partially successful, because despite it working during one-on-one rehearsals, it could not be structured to such an extent that it could be reproduced precisely. Nevertheless, it was indeed work on this performance that showed the way towards the fulfilment of the total act that came with *The Constant Prince*.' (Grotowski Institute 2012f)

and exposed this personal territory, Cynkutis also believed that this emphasis on becoming so open that you are 'no longer acting but just real [ . . . ] like an open nervous system' was not sustainable and ultimately created problems in the work (Cynkutis 1984).

Cynkutis also noted in his journal:

> It is difficult [ . . . ] to draw a distinction between what was the result of Grotowski's own experience and that which was mine in my collaboration with him. [ . . . ] it was not only the method which fused with me but also the teacher [Grotowski]. [ . . . ] There is therefore, a longing for a new method of work in complete independence. (2015a: 161–62)

It was during Cynkutis' absence that work began on what is arguably the Laboratory Theatre's most famous performance: *The Constant Prince*. Rehearsals for *The Constant Prince* continued Grotowski's earlier model—developed during *Faustus*—of working intensively and individually with the actor playing the leading role. This time, Grotowski chose Cieślak to develop the title role of Don Fernando.

Meanwhile, in his work with other regional theatres, Cynkutis realized he would never be able to reach the passion or depth he had found with the Laboratory Theatre. Grotowski, for his part, stayed in touch with Cynkutis and often tried to convince him to return, making clear that both his and Molik's[9] participation was irreplaceable and essential for the company's continued research and performances. In the end, despite any hesitation Cynkutis may have felt about returning, both he and Molik 'greatly respected Grotowski's work' and, in late 1966, they returned at Grotowski's invitation (Cynkutis 1984).

After the premiere of *The Constant Prince*, during the crucible of rehearsals on what was to be the Laboratory Theatre's last theatre piece, *Apocalypsis Cum Figuris* (1969), Grotowski again focused on intensive

9 Zygmunt Molik (Laboratory Theatre actor and voice expert) had also left the theatre during that time.

one-on-one sessions with Cieślak. Cynkutis' journals clearly note his strong feelings about the lack of focus on and development of his own performance work (Cynkutis 2015a: 58–59). It was at this time, I believe, that Cynkutis' search and Grotowski's diverged for the final time, with Cynkutis taking the creative lead in his own explorations and proposals.

From Cynkutis' diary entries, it becomes clear how exciting this new path was:

> I had confided to Bos[10] my need to investigate 'my own creative possibilities'. [ . . . ] The 'challenge' was accepted. A completely unforeseen and inestimably valuable night 'rehearsal'. Something happened that I could thus far only have imagined. [ . . . ] [Later] I led an instructor's course, drawing strength from the night's 'experience'. It seems that everything is working out. It really makes sense. (Cynkutis 2015a: 60–61)

Cynkutis, along with the other members of the Laboratory Theatre, protected their creative process by limiting conversations and writings on the subject.[11] Because of this, we can only conjecture what he found. But given the depth and power of Cynkutis' own work up to that point, and the Laboratory Theatre's engagement of such daring processes as energetic work and trance, I believe that what he initiated at that time was novel, vital, and generative for all of his subsequent work. Whether this was the beginning of his unique vocal work or his ability to animate another's energy—both of which he shared with us in the Hamilton

---

**10** 'Bos' (boss) was the affectionate nickname Laboratory Theatre actors often used when speaking of their director.

**11** There was the belief, based on experience, that if the work was passed along through words alone it led to blocks and hinderances instead of discoveries: 'It was not so much that Grotowski decried the desire to verbalize [ . . . ]. But he was perhaps simply too aware that, if not carried through with the real understanding that comes from direct experience, it can easily lead to the glib formulae he considered so destructive to the delicate growth of actor training' (Kumiega 1985: 46).

workshop—one thing is certain: Cynkutis had found his own path forward, a direction that was yielding important new results.

During the development of *Apocalypsis*, Grotowski realized that tethering his work to the strictures of theatre was limiting his investigations and decided to move in a direction other than the creation of theatre productions. This change of direction crystalized into two distinct lines of exploration: 'paratheatre'[12] and the 'Theatre of Sources'.[13]

Cynkutis did not directly participate in the paratheatrical explorations of the 1970s but, as an active company member, led actor training in Poland and around the world including Italy, Australia, Germany, Austria, and the United States. His visits inspired a variety of acting groups to coalesce and this continued the transmission of the work.

Given his analytical bent, it is no surprise that Cynkutis had an interest in directing and began to direct work internationally. To complement this work, he also pursued a course of studies in directing at the Leon Schiller State Higher School of Film, Television, and Theatre in Łódź, graduating from this programme in 1975.

---

12 Paratheatre was an attempt to transcend the separation that exists between people, including the division between actors and spectators, by creating deep 'meetings' through communal rites and simple interactive exchanges. Intended not to be observed but to be directly experienced, paratheatrical projects were undertaken with participants from around the world. They utilized a combination of ritual, song, and events in nature taking place over an extended period of time. For further explanation, see 'Paratheatre' in Grotowski Institute (2012c).

13 Grotowski described the Theatre of Sources as being 'devoted to those activities which lead us back to the sources of life, to direct, primary perception, to an organic, spring-like experiencing of life, of existence, of presence' (Kumiega 1987: 203). 'In this period of his work [Theatre of Sources], Grotowski traveled intensively through India, Mexico, Haiti and elsewhere, seeking to identify elements of technique in the traditional practices of various cultures that could have a precise and discernible effect on participants' (Wikipedia n.d.). See also Grotowski Institute (2012d).

Among his many directorial projects, of special note is his participation in the 1972–73 season at the Osterwa Theatre in Lublin where he led actor training and conceived and directed the performance of *Jałowa* (Barren, 1973) loosely based on the play *Yerma* (1934) by Federico Garcia Lorca.

Cynkutis was joined for this project by Laboratory Theatre actor Rena Mirecka who performed the title role. It was not only Mirecka's vivid presence in the role that interested Cynkutis. Ever curious, he used this opportunity to experiment with a new process for transmitting acting skills. He commented:

> [ . . . ] for me it was interesting how, through the actor, not through directing, I can stimulate other actors to achieve, very fast, very high skills. [ . . . ] I obliged everyone [the other actors] to be all the time present [on the stage] when work was done so they were able to see how she [Rena] transforms tasks into acting. (Cynkutis 1984)

Along with his directorial and training work outside the company, Cynkutis continued to be entrusted with more authority at the Laboratory Theatre, eventually being given the position of vice director of the theatre from 1978 to 1980. During this time, he was also the director of the Laboratory Theatre's Actor Institute and guided the large paratheatrical event *Tree of People* (1979–80).[14]

---

14 Zbigniew Osiński describes this paratheatrical project as follows:

> *Tree of People* was a work the Laboratory Institute 'performed' with various groups of outsiders throughout 1979 and 1980. It was a work that explored the far reaches of the actor/spectator relationship, the sources of human creativity, and the manner in which individuals can make connections, both physically and non-verbally, with one another. But more than that it seemed to explore what might best be called 'a third realm'-a realm that is neither art on the one hand nor life on the other but rather something else that partakes of both without really being either. (Osiński 1986: 170)

For more on the *Tree of People* project, see Grotowski Institute (2012g).

In the early 80s, during the tumultuous period when martial law was imposed in Poland, it became more difficult for the company to continue their work as freely. There was an ongoing and very real sense of danger as well as the possibility of retaliation if one was perceived as going against the authorities. At that time, Grotowski and the company looked to continue their work abroad, turning their focus to disseminating their theatrical discoveries beyond Poland. Grotowski felt the pressure of the situation so greatly that he sought political asylum in the United States, continuing his work and research at the University of California at Irvine.

Cynkutis travelled extensively in the United States leading training and intensives, directing productions, and eventually taking the position of visiting professor of theatre at Hamilton College in 1982. In this capacity, he continued to develop his ideas and search for ways to transmit the processes he and his colleagues had realized under Grotowski's direction.

In 1984 Cynkutis learnt that, without his knowledge or participation, the company had decided to disband and leave vacant its historic theatre space in Wrocław. At the invitation of the local authorities, Cynkutis returned to Poland to establish Drugie Studio Wrocławskie (The Second Studio of Wrocław) in the former Laboratory Theatre space, starting both a Polish and an international company.

Difficult as it was in Poland at that time, Cynkutis held fast to his dream of creating a theatre that would not only present productions but also guide a new generation of actors. His wish was to provide for the actors and acting companies he had trained internationally a home base where they would be able to present their theatrical research and receive feedback and support.

Cynkutis was in the fullness of his work at the time of his sudden death in 1987. In conjunction with his theatre centre, the Second Studio, he was in close contact with numerous theatre artists and companies throughout the world whom he was continuing to guide and urge forward. Fiercely independent, and working with the self-confidence that defined him, he was directing new work, developing two companies, and continuing to articulate and transmit his discoveries.

Despite the tragedy of his death, what Cynkutis gave continued to be an inspiration. His example and his vision of a theatre that could open doors not only to the natural world but to our deepest selves has remained a challenge and a light to all who knew him.

Thanks to the diligence and devotion of Jola Cynkutis,[15] aided by Khalid Tyabji and Paul Allain, Cynkutis' copious writings and thoughts on theatre training and his reflections on a life in the arts were published. The first volume was published in Polish in 2012 as *Aktor. Animator twórczych procesów* [Actor: Animator of Creative Processes] and the English version, *Acting with Grotowski: Theatre as a Field for Experiencing Life*, was published in 2015.

Cynkutis often spoke to Jola about the last workshop he had led in the US at Hamilton College—of what had been realized there and of the audio recordings that had been made. He wanted the story of this workshop to be brought forward as an important example of his training for actors. This book with its accompanying audio is a testament to Cynkutis' gifts as a teacher and the realization of that wish. It resonates with his voice, his passion, and with the courage that he wished to impart to the next generation of theatre artists. May it unlock missing parts of his legacy and aid others in their search.

---

15 After Cynkutis passed away, his second wife, Jola Cynkutis—actor, director, teacher, and partner in the work—advocated for the establishment of a centre for the preservation of the Laboratory Theatre's workspace and records in the Wrocław space and carried on the work that had been imparted to her by Cynkutis, leading workshops and training in Poland and beyond until her death in 2013.

CHAPTER ONE

# ARRIVAL

## Friday, 15 June 1984

*One day, I will make a theatre that has this opening into nature.*[1]

A deposit was not the only prerequisite when applying for the summer intensive with Zbigniew Cynkutis; a detailed letter of intent was required as well. From the beginning, it was clear that this was not about an exchange of money but about the possibility of a deeper meeting. In my letter, it wasn't difficult to describe why I wanted to study with Cynkutis. My own trajectory as an actor had already shown how vital I felt this work was. Five years earlier, I'd dropped out of Boston Conservatory of Music after completing only two years of a four-year degree programme as a drama major/musical theatre minor and joined the Grotowski-influenced theatre company, Stage One,[2] after seeing their production of *Gertrude og Ophelia* (1975). The devised play was an exploration of a midnight meeting between these two women from Shakespeare's *Hamlet*. The actors who created the piece, Wendy Flagg and Deirdre O'Connell, were on fire. They sang, danced, leapt onto couches brandishing brimming goblets, all the while revealing the intimate landscape of shared pain that lay underneath. I was completely captivated by how alive this work process was and wanted to make it central in my own

---

1 All chapter epigraphs are from Cynkutis' 1984 summer intensive at Hamilton College, Clinton, New York (Cynkutis 1984).

2 Stage One, also called Stage One Theatre Lab, was a Boston-based theatre ensemble directed by Kaleel Sakakeeny during the 1970s and 80s.

creative life. I joined Stage One, training and working with its charismatic director Kaleel Sakakeeny for several years, giving the practice my all. When my collaboration with Stage One ended, I continued searching for a theatre that had an affinity for this kind of work.

I'd known that Cynkutis, a principal member of Grotowski's Laboratory Theatre, had been leading workshops in the United States for some time. One of my Stage One colleagues, Maggie Browning, had been in the ensemble in Pittsburgh that developed the performance piece *DOOR* (1977)[3] under Cynkutis' direction. She had returned changed and inspired. The moment I heard about Cynkutis' summer intensive, I applied.

When I received my letter of acceptance, I was elated. And in June 1984, I packed up the required work clothes (loose pants and a nondescript top) and headed my Volkswagen Beetle to the site of the workshop, Hamilton College in Clinton, New York. I was 29 years old.

Hamilton's sprawling campus is situated high up on a steep hill with vistas of deep woods and fields all around. After I checked in at the dorm rooms assigned to us, I followed the directions on the tiny college map I'd been sent, arriving at last at our meeting place: the faculty apartment of Cynkutis and his wife, Jola (pronounced 'Yola', short for Jolanta). Jola greeted me at the kitchen side door and directed me to follow her to a small living room where a few young people were already perched awkwardly on chairs. Cynkutis was engaging them in conversation, but even in that simple moment, he was vibrant and full of life. He dominated the room simply by his presence. As he turned towards me to include me in the gathering, I was struck by his eyes—so expressive and aware. You

3 *DOOR* was an original theatre piece developed in 1977 from improvisations with a small company of US actors under Cynkutis' direction. After performances at the Mattress Factory in Pittsburgh, where the group was in residence, *DOOR* was performed at the Public Theatre in New York and The New Theatre (TNT) Festival in Baltimore. *DOOR* was produced by Richard Mennen at the University of Pittsburgh with funding from the Pennsylvania Council on the Arts.

knew in an instant that he was *really* seeing you. Really taking you in. He was graced with rugged good looks, a captivating personality, and a relaxed sense of his own body that was part athlete, part finely tuned actor.

After he and Jola made us comfortable in their home and served us something to eat and drink, Jola left the room and Cynkutis began to orient us towards the upcoming workshop. Though his grammar was not always perfect and the accent and cadence of his native Polish language remained, after living several years in the United States, he was almost completely fluent in English and he used it with command. For him language had power; it had import.

I was immediately taken by Cynkutis' humanity. There was a kindness and caring warmth about him that was innate and natural. He seemed energized by our presence—genuinely happy to have us there. In contrast, his conversation was careful, almost guarded. It was clear that precise word choice—what he said and how he said it—was extremely important to him. His effort to communicate was deliberate and active.

We were five in all—gathered in a semicircle around him. Judith Archer was the oldest and, like me, had some familiarity with this kind of theatre. Tall and lean, with close-cropped hair and bright eyes, Judith was just starting out as a theatre teacher and was full of questions. Later in the workshop I would be grateful for her unabashed questioning. So much was revealed because of her deep need to know. There were also three university students: Elizabeth Forrester, Jacqueline (Jackie) Kim, and David E. Saperstein. As I was wondering when the rest of the participants would arrive, Cynkutis announced that our group was complete. I was surprised at the small number, but Cynkutis stated that he had deliberately chosen only five. It later became clear that having such a small number was key to processes that could not otherwise be engaged.

'Is there a certain way you'd like us to refer to you, Professor Cynkutis?' Judith asked. Cynkutis smiled, 'Why don't you call me Zbyszek?' (pronounced 'Zbih-sheck', a familiar form of his first name). As we each began to try out and mispronounce his name, he corrected us and laughed, clearly enjoying the situation. For me, his playfulness brought such welcome lightness. I'm sure I wasn't the only one who was nervous about this first encounter with him.

'How do you spell it?' asked David, gamely. 'I am interested to see how *you* will spell it,' Cynkutis bantered. 'I always learn so much from this kind of creative writing.'

As the evening's conversation progressed, Cynkutis gently probed to see what our theatrical backgrounds might be and hinted at the different approach he would be using. If any of our responses seemed rote or mechanical, he would ask more questions, bringing the conversation to a deeper level. He was provocative not only in what he said but also in how he related to us. His gaze was direct and his physical presence so alive. How often was I really present in a room as he was?

Cynkutis gave us the option of choosing our preferred times to meet: 'You may have noticed there are hours in the day when your focus and energy are the strongest. These are the times we should work.' After some discussion, we chose morning into early afternoon and late afternoon into the evening. He seemed pleased with our choices and I was struck by his concern for our natural rhythms. But then, care and consideration for those who made a commitment to work with him were a hallmark of Cynkutis' work with his students.

'What will we be doing every day?' Elizabeth asked.

'To ask what we will do is a very pragmatic question. It is like to "kill the time". Together we will go on this journey. Many things will be up to you. Who knows what the outcome will be?'

It sounded mysterious, and yet he spoke with precision and careful authority as though he indeed held the key. He released us by saying, 'See you tomorrow morning at the theatre.' And we strolled back together to our first-floor dorm rooms with their wide windows looking out on an open field. The whole encounter had been exhilarating, but my journal entry that night reflects just how confused I was by the absence of articulated goals.

### Journal entry, evening of 15 June 1984

*We haven't even started and my head is already spinning. We undertake a process, we have the groundwork, and yet we don't know the outcome? Is he saying we have an aim, a quest, but no goal? I'm lost. Don't you state what you want out of a theatre piece—that you want to make people laugh or cry or both? Don't you have wishes as far as an audience is concerned? Shouldn't you? But maybe all these questions just show that I have a very preconceived approach. All I know is that I don't know how to get meaning into my art and I have to find a way.*

CHAPTER TWO

# AWAKENING THE BODY AND VOICE

## Saturday, 16 June 1984: Daytime Session in the Theatre

> *We train so that when the opportunity arises, we can make the leap into something new.*

We arrived at Hamilton College's small theatre full of anticipation and the clear, cool energy of morning. It was customary for this kind of work to be done in non-theatrical spaces such as an open room with a bare wooden floor. It seemed odd to be in a theatre with a proscenium stage and row upon row of auditorium style seating; for Grotowski-oriented work this was definitely a non-traditional space! Still, the stage floor was wooden, worn smooth by the passing of many feet, a good base for the explorations to come.

Knowing that exercises could extend for hours, I reminded myself to summon a level of grit for the long haul. From past experience, I knew that the work could be quite demanding and that soon I would encounter my smaller self that wanted to give up after the first difficult hour. The university students hadn't much background in this kind of theatre, but this was not an indicator of how far they could go. Students and the young were welcomed because they didn't have as many preconceptions or years of poor training to overcome.

We were advised to treat our workspace with the utmost respect. Our daily self, idle chatter, and personal emotions were to be left outside the door. Our clothes needed to be plain, comfortable, and easy to move in. Whatever we brought with us was to be piled neatly and placed out of sight.

Newcomers to this way of treating the space, the students at first seemed irritated at not being allowed to sprawl. I remembered a workshop I'd taken with Cynkutis' colleague, Rena Mirecka, who, when she'd seen our piles of belongings strewn everywhere, had gestured at the chaos and called out imperiously, 'Make order!' That reverberating command came to my mind whenever I set up a workspace after that.

Cynkutis cautioned us not to break for questions or make any comments while working. He was trying to establish the right attitude and it was clearly not open to negotiation. Instead of complaints, comments, or cute remarks interrupting the work, there would now be silence, a receptive space in which something new could emerge. We were creating a kind of sacred space around us and that would soon become an invitation to deeper parts of ourselves to be present.

We ascended the steps to the stage barefoot taking with us only our journals. We had been told that there would be times when we could make notes on the exercises and on our process. As Cynkutis introduced our first task, David turned on a small tape recorder. To my surprise, Cynkutis allowed it, his sole condition being that David only record his conversations and training instructions and not the student work itself. 'If you record while we are working,' Cynkutis said, 'it will change everything.' David agreed to this condition and to Cynkutis' stipulation that he give copies to everyone in the workshop for their use. Years later, I would spend countless hours poring over those scratchy tapes, transcribing all that was said at that time.

## Partnering with Objects in the Space

The work began quietly. We were instructed to stand in one place and to reach towards the objects around us and 'touch' them, without ever making actual physical contact with them. The impulse was to begin in the base of the spine and then radiate out to our hand as it reached out to touch an object. Then we would touch the next object with our other hand. Cynkutis demonstrated the exercise, and the relaxed easy motion extending outwards from the core of his body to the objects in the space reminded me of Tai Chi. His movements were never disconnected or jerky as they might have been if they were based on intellectual decisions. They were organic, originating in the body, based and rooted in the body.

We worked with this task for quite a while, but I never felt any overall ease. I was always struggling to decide which object I should reach out to next and this interrupted my flow. I knew it was wrong to use my mind to make the decisions for my body, but I didn't know how to stop it, so I focused instead on the reaching and touching as opposed to the difficult transitions.

Cynkutis introduced another element to our task, 'Voice of Truth'. When we 'touched' the object with our hand, we were to simultaneously touch it with our voice, saying its name, uniting the action of body and voice.

'The voice can touch. This is not imagination. It is a presence in the space, and it needs to be informed with truth or with intention,' Cynkutis said. 'Here we are informing our voice with truth. Simply touch with your voice something in the space and name it.'

We continued to work, touching objects with our voice and naming them. I found this simple exercise to be rich and profound. It stripped away vocal acrobatics and reconnected the doer to childhood honesty in the voice and in the self. The effort to touch the 'other', in this case an object, to simply say an object's name with no emotion or colouring, sourced a reservoir of sound within myself that was undistorted by striving. At the same time, the task required precise attention to my own subtle inner processes. As I repeated each object's name, I tried to sense whether my naming had indeed captured its core, and a feeling of deep communion with each object began to emerge.

Cynkutis then moved us into a more active exercise.

## Vectors[1]

'Whenever and wherever you move, an opposite force exists,' Cynkutis instructed. 'Every action has this partner, this second vector. Vectors can be opposing movements, energies, or forces; they can also be opposing needs. Perhaps it is best to understand it in the body. Find the point at which your body is in balance, then lean and continue to lean until you find the point of greatest difficulty where you are near to falling.'

We did as he suggested and the concept of opposing forces became a dynamic reality as we struggled to stay in balance.

'Now, walk! Walk quickly around the space, changing direction at the last moment,' he coached. 'Surprise yourself!'

We hurried around the space, wheeling quickly to avoid collisions, but though I was in motion, I could feel that I hadn't fully given myself over to the exercise. Cynkutis kept urging us on, calling out, 'Faster! Faster! As fast as you can!' And suddenly, the speed that he insisted on snapped me out of my resistance and into a full experience of the present moment.

'Stop!' We stopped, almost falling over from the impelled motion, balancing precariously. 'Feel your body,' Cynkutis said. 'What is it that keeps you from falling to the ground? Where are the opposing vectors in the body?' He paused, letting us absorb our bodily sensations and then continued, 'Now release this position and walk quickly until I again call *Stop*!'

We continued to explore, following his commands until Cynkutis directed us to no longer rely on him but to stop on our own: 'But do not stop in an easy moment, stop in a moment of difficulty when you are almost not able to do it. Feel the opposing vectors in the body that keep

---

1 'The principle of two vectors is that every movement must contain opposite vectors of force. It is these that distinguish movement from gesture and give you a sense of truth in the movement you are initiating' (Cynkutis 2015a: 101)

you from falling. Release and continue to walk. Use your breath. Do not hold it in.'

We worked vigorously, suddenly changing direction or stopping abruptly. Occasionally I caught a peripheral glimpse of the others, suspended in a moment of tension or lurching forward upon release, bodies in the space engaged in a primal experience of physical vectors.

## The Plastiques

### *Introduction to the plastiques*[2]

Our first training session concluded with learning the plastiques—an important part of the work. These training exercises, developed by Mirecka, are often referred to in the literature on the Laboratory Theatre.[3] They were never approached as mere physical warm-ups; they were used to discover and encounter the self. They would become a physical language with which to dialogue with the space and with each other.

'The whole body needs to be engaged and alive,' Cynkutis said, 'this is not our usual state. One way to develop this is through using the plastiques to activate the different areas and energies of the body by flexing

2 For an in-depth exploration of Cynkutis' teaching of the plastiques, see Cynkutis (2015a: 126–36). For his complete set of exercises designed to warm-up and challenge the body while linking it creatively to images and the environment, see 'Conversations with the Body' (Cynkutis 2015a: 98–153).

3 The Grotowski Institute website features a video of Rena Mirecka improvising within this framework of the plastiques in which the fluidity and presence that this training brings to the body can be clearly seen. In the video, it is possible to discern Mirecka working with a physical image or association as it arises. She departs from the framework as she explores it and then, at the end of the exploration, her body returns to its ongoing grounding in the basic movements of the plastiques (Grotowski Institute 2012e). For an in-depth exploration of Rena Mirecka's development of the plastiques, see Virginie Magnat (2014: 69–72).

and rotating them individually. This then becomes a good source of body-feeling, awakening the body, stimulating each part.'

We stood in a loose circle, with bodies relaxed and a slight bend in our knees as Cynkutis demonstrated the rotation of the head around the neck. He first isolated the circle into four points dropping his head down towards the chest, then back as far as possible, then ear towards each shoulder right and left. We were then to connect these points, rolling our head in a circle to the right and then left with varying degrees of speed and intensity. As I rotated my head towards the back, it felt restricted and tense, so I eased into it slowly and deliberately until, with gentle repetition, it yielded. David had his eyes closed, perhaps to better focus on the sensations, but Cynkutis quickly coached him away from that: 'It is important to be fully present in the space. Do not close the eyes.'

Cynkutis quickly linked our head rotation to an image. 'Imagine that there is a long spoon coming out of the top of your head. With this spoon you are stirring the universe!' Galvanized by the image we were now fully engaged in the rotation.

Cynkutis then coached us in the plastiques for other parts of the body. For each area, we began by flexing strongly to the four points of the circle: front, back, right and left, going so far that we encountered and engaged the body's resistance. These individual positions could be used later when in dialogue with a partner or the space. First we isolated the chest and later the hips, rotating them in circles around the axis of the spine. Cynkutis instructed us to always include engagement of the space. As we rotated each part, we were to take in the space by reaching out to the wall or objects around us with each rotation. We were cautioned to always work with eyes open so that we did not retreat into an inner world.

The knees were rotated by bending them forward, circling them to the right and then back and straight before rotating them to the front again. The feet were lifted one by one and rotated around the ankle joints. The shoulders were rotated both individually and together around the shoulder joints. The elbow (with the corresponding hand held by the opposing hand) circled an imaginary point like the swing of a jump rope. After shaping the hands into fists, they were rotated around the wrist joint activating that area. For the plastique of the hands, the fingers initiated the circle. Beginning with the pinkie, the fingers were curled in towards the palm, with each digit extended one by one, scooping out the surrounding space.

I found the elbow plastique confusing, so Cynkutis demonstrated it more slowly. 'With your left hand, loosely hold the fingers of your right hand, stabilizing it, then initiate the elbow rotation. Elbow bent, raise your right elbow up and then in towards your body as you straighten it. The elbow then comes down closer into your body, then back up to its bent position, completing the circle.'

I clumsily executed the motion, frowning with concentration. When Cynkutis saw that my main focus was on following instructions, he countered: 'Perhaps this is not the best approach. Better that you feel the impulse that leads the elbow to movement. Remember, these actions are not physical exercises but sources of images and associations. For now, your elbow is a snake with its beginning in the spine. Sometimes it is shy, sometimes bold, exploring the world.'

This image freed up my work with elbow and arm, and I made a mental note: focus on the movement not the mechanics; find and follow an image, not the empty form.

We were told to begin each plastique slowly, establish the movement and then play with it, changing direction and speed, experiencing how these differences affected us. As we became aware of areas where we felt resistance, we were to increase our speed and 'attack' that held place with the rotation, creating a release of energy. We were cautioned to feel the impulse of movement from the base of the spine, not the limbs. The life of the spine would be a uniting element, aiding us in the transition from one plastique to another.

As I began the plastiques, I could clearly feel the different energies of each part of the body: the thin, high vibration of the neck; the lazy arcing of the hips; the articulation of the hands. It was a joy to meet each body area on its own terms, though as I increased the speed of the circles, I often lost touch with the distinct qualities I had just encountered. I wasn't sure if I was shocked out of sensing by the increase in motion or by my insecurity as to what I should be looking for or finding.

### *Improvisation: A river of images and associations*

Cynkutis aided our search by taking us deeper into the purpose of this training:

> Although we begin with physical movements, circles which rotate the body's joints, we are looking for the life of the body: impulses—spontaneous acts arising organically in the body through the body. As these elements grow, change, and transform, they take the body into a stream of continuous movement with its source in the spine—never without the spine. This is different from a warm-up which isolates different parts of the body. Here there is always the connection with the spine and being open to what arises. With the plastiques, if you are circling the hands, the whole body is engaged; your whole body is for that rotation of the hand. And there is no focus on emotion. To do that brings with it what I call a 'pumping of emotion'. That is like a kind of emotional masturbation that forces the feelings to be present which is exactly the wrong direction. Begin again and when you feel warm, communicate with another person through the movements. Try to do something to them with these elements.

We began to dialogue with each other using the plastiques. As we worked, our body configuration, the speed of our movement, our closeness to or distance from another, our experience of the space and innumerable other factors caused images and associations to arise. These spontaneous and naturally occurring images and memory fragments became the basis for interaction with each other and with the environment. Because these discoveries came from the movements of our physical bodies, they were immediately expressive.

An example of an image arising from a movement: rotating an elbow rhythmically and with a lot of engagement of the forearm might remind one of how it felt to pull something and might provoke an image of drawing water from a well. With exploration, this first image might lead to a deeper discovery about that action, a memory or more of a sense of story surrounding it. For another example, while rotating the shoulders backwards, repeating a movement from the base of the spine up through both shoulders and down the arms might lead one to the image that the arms were beating like the wings of a bird in flight. Or, rotating the hands, with arms stiff and straight out from the body while backing away from a partner, might provoke the association that one was trying to 'eliminate' that person or defend oneself against them. Letting an image that arose in partner-work continue and develop might lead one to discover that it was linked either to a memory from the past or an impulse in relation to the partner.

The plastiques were a base to improvise from and a grounding place to return to, keeping the work linked to the body. Whatever arose, whatever impulses came, became the present-moment foundation for 'dialoguing' with partners and elements in the space.[4]

I had attempted to interact with partners using the plastiques in training sessions before and had always found it challenging. Occasionally an image or association would appear, but it often seemed weak or too ordinary, so I didn't stay with it or explore it for long. My desire was to encounter strong and unmistakable impulses, but that goal seemed far

---

4 For an informed explanation of the vocabulary used by Grotowski such as impulse, association, score, and sign, see James Slowiak and Jairo Cuesta (2007: 64–69).

beyond me. In retrospect, I now understand that staying with whatever is arising organically and allowing it to develop is one of the most important tasks.

I continued with the exercise, trying to communicate with the others and keep a steady stream of impulses moving in my body, but every time I transitioned from one plastique to another, I couldn't find the flow. My tendency was to make a mental decision that it was time to move on to another rotation instead of remaining in the stream of movements. My body felt disjointed and separate from me, like something I was clumsily managing. I was so preoccupied with doing the exercise right that it dominated my approach, making me forceful and unreceptive. All the while my mind was active, simultaneously observing and questioning: Was that an impulse? What is an impulse? In all likelihood, my drive to do the exercise right and my tendency to scrutinize were causing me to pass over whatever was there to be discovered.

In the work, the phrase *via negativa*[5] often emerges. The philosophy behind it is that if we rid ourselves of our blocks, of whatever has been layered onto ourselves, then our natural spontaneity and organic impulses will emerge. What would be required to rid me of my vigilant and overactive mind?

Everyone was exploring the task as best they could while trying to stay in relation to the others. Judith's focus was powerful. She went straight for engagement with no concern what her relation to her own body might be. Jackie's movements were controlled, almost dance-like. Elizabeth tended to hang back from engagement, as did David. He

---

5 Grotowski's explanation of *via negativa* is as follows: 'The education of an actor in our theatre is not a matter of teaching him something; we attempt to eliminate his organism's resistance to this psychic process. The result is freedom from the time-lapse between inner impulse and outer reaction in such a way that the impulse is already an outer reaction. Impulse and action are concurrent: the body vanishes, burns and the spectator sees only a series of visible impulses. Ours then is a *via negativa*—not a collection of skills but an eradication of blocks' (1968: 16–17).

seemed uncertain, perhaps even fearful when I interacted with him and it made me want to dominate him with my stronger energy. That was the closest thing to an impulse that I had.

Cynkutis watched us as we worked. The quality of his presence steadied me. I tried to stay with my body as best I could but soon I was distracted again, this time worrying whether I was doing the exercise well enough for him.

We broke for several moments and, as we rested, Cynkutis carefully searched for the right way to reach us. When he finally spoke, he questioned the whole model of striving for complete, unassailable success in our performance work. What he said was a direct challenge to us all:

> **[Audio #1]** It is so important in acting to forget or to 'un-train'—maybe that is better—we have to 'un-train' ourselves from wanting to show perfection or beauty [on the stage]. Perfection is boring and perfection is like a weapon. The more perfect you are the less possibility you have to contact me. Because if you are perfect it means I am not so perfect. If you show me how perfect you are, I must feel guilty that I am not so perfect. So instead of creating a bridge into human relationships, you are breaking them. **[End Audio #1]**

At first, I thought he was referring to Jackie's controlled, dance-like movements, but then realized I myself had been focused on trying to execute the task perfectly in order to gain his approval. This had kept me from being present to my partner and to what was arising in my own work. Cynkutis continued:

> In this work, it is not that *I* am important. I am a servant to the task. I believe that from myself are coming values, not that *I* am valuable.
>
> In the moment when I am starting the performance on the stage, I feel like a servant. I feel like a servant towards my partner also. And, because I see myself as a servant for my partner, I feel good. I don't feel bad. I serve my workshop abilities for my

> partner or partners with whom I am working. They serve their abilities, discipline and knowledge for me, whom they are acting with. We, together on the stage, are serving ourselves for the audience. But it is not a special effort towards the audience, only a phenomenon that we do serve one another makes it a service for the audience. With this freedom I can feel my courage and I can feel my dignity, because the profession of acting has incredible dignity. Do not 'show yourself' but serve the task at hand, serve your partner.

I felt grateful for his insight. Involvement with the task and with our partner was what was important, not trying to 'show' ourselves or execute the exercise 'perfectly'. I resolved to focus solely on his proposals without worrying about the outcome or how I looked in the process. That much I could try to do. Simplify my focus. Serve the task at hand. Serve my partner.

CHAPTER THREE

# NATURAL SOURCES

## Saturday, 16 June 1984: Evening Session in the Theatre

> *Art comes from nature, from this living source.*

This evening, Jola, Cynkutis' wife and partner in the work, joined us at the theatre. Jola had boyish charm, taut, quicksilver energy, and a bubbling laugh. It was usual for her to actively assist in the workshops, galvanizing the participants and demonstrating the exercises. But because she was preparing for their imminent return to Poland, there were only a few occasions she could be with us. Jola had a lilt in her walk and power and precision in her work. I was lucky enough to partner with her on some of the exercises.

### Partner Work / Vectors of Support

'Find a partner and lean your back against them, feeling the warm area of contact where your bodies meet,' Cynkutis said. He elaborated:

> As you lean, find the point at which you and your partner are supporting each other's weight. Do not use the bony parts of the skeleton as they will stop this feeling of togetherness. Using only the soft parts of your body continue to move supporting each other's weight in various ways. Create between you the vectors that are needed so that the other does not fall. Sometimes you support and sometimes your partner is supporting you. Where is the point of balance between you? Remember to keep always this warm area of contact as you move. You can speak through

> your back to your partner. Name what comes to your senses, for example: 'Your back is lifting me,' 'Your shoulder is warm.' Say what you experience and touch your partner with your voice.

Quietly sensual, this twisting, twining encounter with each other's body grounded us in the present moment and brought us into direct communion with our partner.

### Sourcing Elements in Nature

Cynkutis indicated that we should take a seat in the auditorium as he introduced the next task:

> Now we will continue work with partners in a different way. I am going to give to each of you a different phenomenon of nature. Two opposing vectors in nature. For instance: one of you is 'Heat' and the other is 'Cold.' Speak to each other, relate to each other as these elements. Touch each other with your voice and your touching is 'Heat' or it is 'Rain.' The source of your voice is this natural element. Think only that. You are not the voice; this element in nature is the voice. When you speak, your text can be the story of your element. What is happening? Speak as your element. Improvise. It is not so important what you say. What is important is that you touch your partner and relate to your partner as this element. Take it all the way.

He called Jola and I onto the stage to work. She was given 'Mountain' and I was given 'Valley' to source. Jola took a strong position facing me. Her cropped, blonde hair was haloed by the theatre lights. I could feel the strong presence of Cynkutis and the others watching from the darkened theatre but I brought my attention back to the task, resolving to focus only on his directive: 'You are not the voice; this element in nature is the voice.' I sank down into my image of 'Valley', feeling it as a dark pull in the solar plexus. Jola's clear voice rang out, the voice of the heights with the world at its command. As she spoke, I felt imprisoned by her force, reduced to a shadow before this 'Mountain' she was creating. I responded from my sunken area, from this heavy, submerged place of 'Valley' that I was sourcing and every sound I made became a subterranean effort to subvert this mountain, to pull it down. Jola responded strongly and a battle began between these two opposing vectors. Each of us trying to dominate. The task took all my concentration to sustain and when we finished, I was physically and emotionally drained.

Jackie and David were called onto the stage and given 'Sun' and 'Rain' as their elements, but they weren't able to commit to or source the raw power of their images. Their voices and bodies remained ordinary and the improvisation stayed in the realm of clever wordplay. Others were called up to work, but the voice/image connection did not transform them either, at least not at this time.

Cynkutis then brought us together for a group improvisation in which we were all waiting for a train at a railway station. The nature element we had just explored was to be the basis for our character. 'Your vectors will be the desires and needs of your character opposed by the needs of others,' he directed.

I was immediately thrown off. What kind of strong desires could this element of 'Valley' have in a railway station? I didn't know what to hold onto to keep my element alive and, because Jola hadn't been able to stay for this exercise, I didn't have our opposition to orient me. Seeing our haphazard efforts, Cynkutis completely changed his approach.

## Opposing Vectors: Darkness and Light

Cynkutis turned off all the peripheral lights in the theatre leaving only two spotlights. They cut through the darkness, creating two pools of light on the stage. His words guided us into the task:

> The actor is the most important element in theatre, but light is the second. Tonight, we will explore that relationship. Choose one of these lights and place yourself in relation to it. Go towards

the light with one part of your body and then find how another part of your body pulls you away and towards the darkness. Search for what causes these impulses of 'towards' and 'away'. Sometimes movement to the light is stronger, at other times it is the call of the shadow. Explore these opposing vectors of darkness and light with your body.

Simple as it was, this exercise powerfully engaged the imagination, drawing us into a metaphorical landscape of opposing forces of darkness and light. I began to see myself as a kind of plant, nurtured by and yearning for the light before being pulled down again towards darkness and the void. A primitive struggle began wherein sometimes I strained upward towards the light and at other times was overpowered by the darkness or sought the blessing of rest. The story played out again and again, conjuring different images and associations, and, as it did, I began to feel an ache in my middle that was not just muscular but was an inner sensation created by the tension of these opposing forces.

As the day's work ended, Cynkutis surprised us by handing out copies of the play *Long Day's Journey into Night* by Eugene O'Neill.

'As our workshop progresses, I want you to work not only with improvised words but with a text. Tonight, choose a section from the play. You can choose a monologue or, if you have someone you would like to work with, it can be a scene,' he stated.

Elizabeth and Jackie exchanged glances, excited by this possibility. 'When do you want it memorized?' Jackie asked.

'Memorizing is not the way we will approach the text. Not even in conventional theatre should you rush to put written words into your mind too quickly. The body will discover, the voice will discover, and you will crush all of this if you lock artificial rhythms into your head,' Cynkutis cautioned. He ended our session by again focusing us on the task: 'Select for yourself a text that speaks to you. You may not even be able to say why it attracts you. Search and see what you will find.'

I was excited by this inclusion of work with a script. Later that night, as I skimmed through the play, I came across a gripping monologue by Mary Tyrone, the drug-addicted mother. Mary speaks to her servant Cathleen of her younger days. Her happy memories of playing the piano alternate with the repulsion she now feels as she looks at her crippled hands, twisted and deformed by arthritis. These sharply opposing experiences of her hands were like the vectors Cynkutis had so strongly emphasized. I carefully wrote out the monologue on a single sheet of paper. Then I folded it and placed it near my clothes for tomorrow's session. In days to come, it would become tattered and limp from being gripped so tightly as I worked.

Before heading to bed, I picked up my journal. After this full day of work, I was elated.

### Journal entry, evening of 16 June 1984

*It feels so right to be working with an image as we did today, so different from anything I've ever done before. I especially love sourcing the voice as though it is an element of nature. It was freeing because what to concentrate on was so specific and clear it absorbed my mind. Maybe I'm in the beginning stages of finding a way to be a servant to the task. The pure enjoyment and release I'm finding in this work is incredible.*

CHAPTER FOUR

# VOICE OF THE TREE

## Sunday, 17 June 1984: Daytime Session in Nature

*We can drink from nature. Get secrets from it.*

'Today, nature will be our laboratory!' Cynkutis announced with delight. He led us out of the theatre and up to the crest of a small promontory. In the distance was a horizon of rolling, forested hills.

### Partnering with the Landscape

Encouraging us to stand beside him, facing the great expanse, Cynkutis said:

> Choose something in the distance and move with your body towards it to 'touch' it. Your hand is an extension of that impulse, extending the movement of your body, reaching out to touch. Trace the shape you are reaching towards with your whole body until something else in the landscape calls to you. Continue moving and 'touching' led by what you find in the landscape.

He moved over to one side to watch our work leaving us to the task. For almost an hour, we brought ourselves into relation with nature using this exercise, intertwining our movements with trees, clouds, and hills.

Cynkutis beckoned to us to follow him and made his way purposefully down the meandering face of the promontory, moving from foothold to foothold with youthful athleticism. We skittered down after him and followed him over to an imposing tree at the edge of a large field.

No other tree was in sight. This one had probably been left to provide shade for the cows after the rest of the forest had been cut down for pastureland. It dominated the landscape with its spreading branches and heavy trunk, thick with age.

## Sourcing the Voice of the Tree

Cynkutis gestured to us to gather around the tree and said:

> With your body, take on one of the vectors that you see in this tree. Then find a vector in the tree that opposes it and create that with your body. With the life force of these two vectors in your body, explore the tension they create. Then explore another set of vectors within the tree. Find the vectors that for you create the essence of this tree.

We began our work by quickly falling into static representations, spreading our arms like branches. 'Vectors, not Posing!' Cynkutis called out. 'Find the forces that create strength, reaching, standing. Find what can happen in your spine. Use the vectors to keep it alive.'

We became more animated now, trying with the core of our bodies to find the dynamic tensions within the tree. We tried to not only take on the shapes but somehow to intuit the forces behind them, recreating those living vectors in our own bodies. After some time, Cynkutis urged us in a new direction: 'Gather together now and become a living, moving sculpture of this tree. Find its voice, a voice that is made up of many voices, many branches, and many vectors. Words may come to you like "sky" or "rain".'

We came close together, interweaving, trying to bring the tree to life. Its presence and our experience with its vectors fed our work, bringing with it a deeply focused communion. Far from being self-conscious individuals, it felt as though we were now one entity channelling the tree's essence. The sounds and words that came to us were both surprising and unexpected like fragmentary utterances from an ancient prayer.

When the improvisation had come to its natural end, Cynkutis gathered us at the base of the great tree to talk. 'The origins of theatre are very ancient, and they are full of mystery,' Cynkutis paused for emphasis and then continued:

> Shamans, for instance, were called on to make rain—or make a journey to another world and bring back a vision. This vision would then be acted out by the people and would become an important ritual. A ritual that was also theatre. The shaman/actor was also a priest and fulfilled a need in the society. Why should we make theatre whose purpose is only about making money? It can be the case that theatre today fulfils an important function. If it is not the case then why should we do it?

'Doesn't theatre that's political fulfil an important need?' Judith asked.

> No, Judith, the idea is not to create theatre for politics. Art used for politics is propaganda. But we'll talk more another time. Let us begin the last work for today. Each of you now, go into the woods and search until you find your tree. The one that speaks to you. It can be that it even is waiting for you. Once you have found it, explore its vectors with your body. Not only the shapes; find what are the opposing tensions that make up this tree. Take time. Take time. When you find the vectors that for you are the essence of the tree, let the voice of the tree come from that place.

With those words of advice, he left us to our task.

It felt exhilarating to set off into the woods alone; to have a reason to explore nature as a theatre artist was heavenly. The day was warm and there was no breeze, just stillness and heat. A small birch tree caught my eye and I circled it, mirroring the vectors I saw in it with my body. But, after a time, I felt disinterested and reasoned that the problem was not my attention but that this tree didn't really capture my imagination.

I set out deeper into the woods, part hunter, part lover, on the lookout for the tree whose essence would speak to me. No tree appealed to my senses with any force or significance until, at last, I found one that stood a bit alone. It was graceful and strong with clearly articulated limbs. Though I didn't know what kind of tree it was, I spontaneously decided it was an elm, like the great tree that used to stand beside my grandmother's sprawling farmhouse in Maine. I walked slowly around the tree, letting its presence sink in. I stood before it, taking it in through my body, locating vectors and finding their opposing forces, moving, changing, remembering Cynkutis' words, 'Vectors, not Posing!' As I worked, I felt energized. There was something intuitively right about this tree's presence, and it aided my work.

Once I had the vectors strongly established, it was time to find the voice of the tree, but even though I seemed to be alone in the woods, I still felt inhibited about speaking out loud. There was something about the articulation of sound that made me feel as though I would be over-stepping a social boundary. I didn't want to be judged by potential passers-by. I had to banish those thoughts, focus my will, and attend to the vectors in my body and in the tree before me. Then I discovered a second block. I could feel myself jump to a conception of the voice of the tree before I had completely sourced it. My mind wanted to imagine and decide what this tree would sound like instead of staying with the vectors and seeing what would emerge. I had to deliberately leave the safety of this habitual response and stay in a state of not knowing, trying to remain true to the essence of the tree and have the voice come from that. I tried to sink down into the root of the opposing vectors and find a pool of sound there. Sound did eventually emerge—softly at first and then with increased strength. The first word that came was 'elm'. I repeated it again and again, savouring the sound. I continued to work, keeping the vectors active, exploring sound, alone, in the woods, in front of this living tree.

CHAPTER FIVE

# THE STAGE AS AN ENVIRONMENT

## Sunday, 17 June 1984: Evening Session in the Theatre

*For the good actor, the stage, like nature, is an environment.*

This evening, Cynkutis had the backstage door open. Through it, we could see several trees framed by the beauty of twilight. After our heat-filled day, the stillness of the space and the approaching dusk created silence in us all.

### Embodying the Tree

Cynkutis' voice was soft as he focused us on this evening's work:

> Remember this afternoon when you went to find your tree? Through your work you are going to bring that presence here. Search where your tree will be in this space. Find the place that is right. When you have found it, explore again the vectors of the tree. The voice of the tree comes from there. Give voice to this tree.

This exercise reminded me of Carlos Castaneda's book *The Teachings of Don Juan* (1968) in which the old sorcerer tells his apprentice to sense different areas in order to find the place that is his power spot. Cynkutis' instructions were also calling on a deeper, more intuitive layer of the psyche.

I chose the spot for my tree by first avoiding the areas that didn't feel right. Eventually, I settled on a quiet space only a few feet from the back wall of the theatre, but far enough from the others that I had a sense of my own realm. To this day, I remember that exact place on the stage and how it made me feel. It brought strength and grounding to all of my subsequent work.

I began by exploring the vectors I had discovered earlier in the day, but when I tried to source the voice of the tree, I found that I still wanted to pre-conceive it. To sidestep that tendency, I focused not only on the vectors but on conjuring an inner presence of the tree by sourcing my memory of it. From this place, with a kind of open attention, I allowed sound to emerge.

The word that came was the same that had emerged in the woods—a simple naming of 'elm'—but the sound was unlike anything I could ever recall producing. It rolled out slowly like a mantra, unexpectedly deep and resonant. Around me were the rooted bodies and upwardly twisted arms of the others. An elemental hum began among us with eerie whispers and truncated phrases as trees found their voices. Words like 'rain' or 'to the light' filled the space.

Cynkutis gently guided our explorations from the side: 'Now keep the voice of the tree and relate to others from this place. If you have the impulse, you may also move.' As a tree, moving was clearly something I did not want to do! But by strongly holding on to the vectors or returning to them when I felt the essence of my tree slipping away, I was able to take in others and begin to experience what our relationship might be.

'Still keeping the tree in your body, take the wooden boxes and construct for yourselves a living room,' Cynkutis directed. We pulled the large cubes and rectangles at the back of the stage forward, forming them into blockish sofas and tables.

'How do you feel about the others in this space? Is this your space or their space? Relate to them with the vectors from your tree and with your voice,' Cynkutis coached.

I stood at the edge of our 'living room' and turned towards the others, trying to stay true to this character developed from nature. Slowly but surely a persona, shy but strong, rooted in this tree-self began to emerge. Whenever I felt lost, I returned to the vector work and my memory of the tree.

## A State of Readiness

After a break in which we were allowed to make notes, Cynkutis challenged us again. As he spoke, he walked around the space. The fluidity of his movement, combined with the feeling of coiled intention underneath, was like a preface to the work to come:

> How can your body be ready to move and respond instantly? In this exercise, we will prepare our bodies to be in such a state of 'alarm and readiness'. Even when you sit, you should be ready to respond at any moment. Practise sitting down and then standing. Search to find a way that you can always move quickly and easily from one position to another. Also practise lying down, then standing up. What in us needs to be alert and alive for this to happen effortlessly? Physically and psychologically!

This exercise, so vigorous and so difficult to achieve, filled the theatre with energy. It was clearly not just a physical task but also a psychological challenge. Something in me kept looking for a break, but the rest that I wanted was, in fact, a collapse, a removal from the present moment, not the alert repose that was needed. To counter it, I kept moving, but my energy was superficial and frenetic. Perhaps it could be called active, but it was not a deep state of readiness.

I wondered how everyone else was doing, but when I tried to observe their work, it immediately took me out of my own centre. Still, the feeling in the space was electric. Perhaps this was not the energy Cynkutis was looking for, but we were on the hunt and activated by the task.

When Cynkutis ended the exercise, we were completely exhausted and collapsed on the floor. As we rested, catching our breath, he told a story that dramatized one of the many metaphors he used to teach his approach to acting.

## Conversation: The Stage as an Environment

**[Audio #2]** All over the world there are butterflies which are huge, their wings are incredibly colourful: red and yellow, yellow and black, black and pink, pink and green. Wherever they land, you see them. When they fly, they fly slowly. They fly heavy. They don't fly fast. They don't change directions rapidly. They can fly from tree to tree, from grass to grass and there is no bird or animal which is hunting for them because each animal, each bird, knows that the taste of this butterfly is awful. They are dying, not killed as food for another animal; they are dying because they are old. After they die, they become useful, because they fertilize the soil, so it is the only practical use of those butterflies.

But there are millions of other kinds of butterflies. Sometimes you see—on the grass—'Oh, something moved!' You try to see but you don't see. But something moved! You are coming closer and you see a butterfly which looks exactly like grass. 'Something moved through the air! No, I don't see it.' No, but if you focus your eyes, you see a flying butterfly but it has almost no colour on its wings; if you focus your eyes, you can see maybe one black dot. 'Oh, yeah! Smart! It looks like air.' 'Smart! It looks like grass.' Another one—'Smart, it looks like a rock.' Another one—yellow. 'Smart! It looks like a yellow flower.' And these butterflies never fly slowly; they always fly quick, and they hide themselves because each animal, each bird, knows that they taste incredibly good. They are food, good food, for thousands of other species. That's why their life is dangerous. They have to find these forms of camouflage, how to adapt, how to assimilate with nature.

Bad acting is like those big butterflies. Colourful, heavy, slow, or fast it is always much too much. Good acting is like those other butterflies. If they will sit on a rock, they look like a rock. If they will sit on grass, they look like grass.

For good actors, the stage is an environment it is not a place to show one's own self. Like for those good butterflies, nature is not a stage to show one's own self but a place to feel confident, to feel safe. For good actors, knowledge about lights, props, furniture, costume, voice, and body is not to show [oneself], but to feed from this environment, to drink from the environment, and to assimilate this environment organically into the body—through the body.

So this is a really excellent example, in sense of acting and in sense of attitude, what makes good and bad acting. **[End Audio #2]** Now, an exercise . . . .

## Sourcing Objects and Others Using Vectors

Cynkutis walked to the middle of the stage and carefully took in the surroundings. He then indicated that we should join him, gesturing to what was around us: 'As you see an object in the room, a piece of furniture, something on the wall, take its vectors into your body, become this object and move to it. Then choose another object, take its vectors and move towards it. Continue working in this way.'

With real objects to focus us, the exercise gained an immediate intensity. As I took in each new object, I tried to register not only its obvious shape but to intuit its deeper vectors—the dynamic, energetic forces that give it life. I felt galvanized as though in the process of attempting to become the object, I also received energy from it.

‘Now the place that you are in is a funeral parlour. See something in this room that makes you sad or causes you pain and move towards it,’ Cynkutis suggested.

Now I was lost. I didn’t know what to focus on or how to find an object that would affect me emotionally. Cynkutis didn’t give us any clues either. If we were going to find anything, it would have to come from our own inner depths, our own secrets and associations. I tried many objects, but nothing affected me. Later, when I looked back on what I had done, I realized I had spent all my time trying to *imagine* I was in a funeral parlour and no time *living* it. Perhaps it was because I didn’t summon any of my own memories to feed my imagination. But I also did not simply accept the truth of Cynkutis’ proposition—‘You are in a funeral parlour’—and, with my eyes opened by that reality, find my object. Usually, when Cynkutis spoke to us strongly and clearly, it was as though he could create the situation by his certainty, by the way he gave a directive. But, in this improvisation, I simply could not find my way and I was not the only one.

Cynkutis saw that we were floundering and introduced a simpler approach: ‘Please find a place somewhere on the stage.’ We all moved to various areas. He continued: ‘Begin by focusing on one person. It does not matter if they are looking at you or not. Take on the vectors in their body and then move towards him or her. Once you are close, find a different person and take on their vectors. Move towards that partner. Continue moving and changing partners.’

I found this exercise powerful but strange. We were intuiting and interpreting each other on a deep, physical level but it was psychological as well. It felt like I was deliberately crossing certain social boundaries, revealing what I thought about others in a bare and too-honest way, mirroring one person’s slouch, another’s coldness and rigid frame. I was glad when the exercise was over; like forced intimacy, it felt quite unnerving.

## Voice and Intention

Cynkutis gathered us together, and the look in his eyes, both resolute and strong, quieted us. From the way he spoke, it became clear that our next task was of deep importance to him:

> The voice affects the audience; it affects our partner. It has a function and it needs to have its source in truth or in an intention. Certainly, our voice needs truth, but it needs purpose as well. For this task, we are going to give our voice *intention*. I want you to do something to furniture and to objects in the space with your voice. Try to move them or caress them. How specific can you be? Use the breath, do not hold it in. Keep the impulses flowing. For your text you may use the alphabet, counting, naming of the object, or a sentence from the monologue you have chosen from *Long Day's Journey into Night*.

This exercise gave me a clear purpose. With every particle of my being, I tried to affect the objects in the space with my voice. At first, I counted, and later I worked with lines from my monologue, constantly surprised at how expressive the voice was when there was absolute focus on the task. Different intentions revealed different and unusual meanings in the text. Cynkutis elaborated on the task energizing us with passion and purpose:

> Continue this work with a partner. Try to do something to your partner with your voice. Be specific. Engage your body but do not make gestures to represent something. That is like being captured by those forms of stage acting which are like models you can imitate. Acting is not a source of models or ready solutions from the stage: pictures or shapes. No! If something becomes a model, it means it is dead. It is like a dead gesture. Gesture is empty and certainly acting should never be facial gesture, it comes from the body.

> Acting is a source of energy. The actor is a generator. He is able to produce, evoke energy. Search for the energy from which gesture can come. *Do* something with your body and voice! If you wish someone to go away, 'Go away!' comes from the toes. The voice is an extension of the body.

I worked as specifically as I could, choosing an intention and trying with all my might to affect my partner. I was amazed at the amount of concentration and effort it took. It was a full-out attempt to do the impossible.

Cynkutis then took part, working with me as his partner, demonstrating this exchange of vocal impulses. Even though he spoke in Polish, the force and specificity of his intentions were still clear. He commented on what he was doing in the exchange: 'As I work, I am trying to do something specific to my partner with my voice. For instance: lift my partner off the floor; push them back. Continue with various partners with the aim to do something to them with your voice. Have a clear intention.'

We continued our efforts until he ended the session. He was clearly pleased with what we had done:

> [Audio #3] So what you did, you were like those good butterflies because you didn't think how to show your voice: you served yourself for your voice, you served your body. Each of you working, talking, whatever your text, your whole body was talking, from feet up to the top of your head. Your body was involved to create this dance. That's why the *impulse* which you gave to the partner was not only the meaning of the sentence, but it was this energy from the body going from your body to the body of the partner which is much more important than the text. Because it is non-verbal communication at the same time that it's verbal communication. But it's impossible to play if we don't feel *function of the voice*. If we don't know *why* we are talking, *what* we want to achieve, *what* we want to change, *what* we want

to get or to give. So, each of you was alive. Talking with your whole body engaged. There was not even one moment when you thought what to do with your hands or legs because they were not important. What was important was your concentration and how you *seek* to do whatever you selected for your voice. Beautiful concentration. **[End Audio #3]**

### Journal entry, evening of 17 June 1984

*Another great day! I love this work with a specific task or image. Even the work with the tree which could be abstract became concrete. When Zbyszek asked us to enter the living-room environment as the tree, I felt freed by the source work done before and a full set of 'character impulses' came into play. The later work with seeing an object taking on its characteristics and then going to it, this kind of mimicry I find incredibly empowering. Look at all these tools!*

CHAPTER SIX

# OWNING THE BODY

## Monday, 18 June 1984: Daytime Session in the Loft

> *Vectors bring a strong and immediate connection to the partner. For individual actors* [ . . . ] *they bring presence.*

Our daytime session was in the 'Loft', a large open room with wooden floors and high windows looking out over the tree-lined paths of the campus. The weather was hot and oppressively humid; even with the windows open there was no breeze.

We began with warm-ups of our own choosing. I focused on moving through the plastiques, seeing what would arise, but I wasn't really engaged in any overarching image or intention and the whole attempt was flaccid leaving me completely preoccupied with my thoughts. I glanced surreptitiously around the room. The warm-ups could hardly be called physical. Several people were making vague motions, someone else was sitting completely still. The overall feeling was of some dream-like inner work, an avoidance of physicality. I thought I was on the right track by working with the plastiques but in reality, I was also escaping by continually glancing at the others.

Our dreamy warm-ups prompted Cynkutis to begin the day with a strong physical approach. He started by telling us why it is important to push ourselves beyond our usual limits:

> If you do not train, if you do not invest anything in yourself to develop your skills, you cannot take a risk. The body, on the very first step of each effort, will show how weak it is. The voice, in

the very first moment of improvisation, when it will be necessary to do something other than what you know from your life and from your habits, will say, 'No! Do not try! You will hurt your vocal cords!' In this way, you will be kept on the track of everything that is familiar, and your imagination will not be free to take you anywhere new.

This morning we will train in such a way that we challenge the body.

## Gymnastics

### *Headstands, Shoulder Stands, and Forward Rolls*

We have learned different ways of exploring the body, for instance the plastiques. These are never just physical exercises; they are used to encounter ourselves, to interact with our environment, and to communicate. Another way to change our usual way of relating is by using headstands, shoulder stands, and forward rolls as a vocabulary to dialogue with one another and the space. They can also be used to activate the energy of the body.

Cynkutis demonstrated the headstand.

FIGURE 3

> Make a triangular base with forearms flat on the floor; hands clasped together become the top of the triangle. Place the back of your head upside down between the clasped hands. Legs are together and straight out in a line from your body—hips high. Feet are flexed and you are on the balls of the feet. Walk your feet towards your head, and as you walk, your back also rises straight up from the floor. When the weight and the point of balance shifts to your torso, lift your feet off the ground and raise your legs into a crouched position, knees in towards the chest. From that position, slowly raise your legs upward until you are in a headstand.[1]

We watched him execute the form with precision, strength, and grace. None of us seemed to be in proper physical shape for this.

Cynkutis continued to demonstrate:

> Once you are in the headstand, hold the body calm and balanced and try to relieve the left arm of the need to support it. Stabilize your body and do the same with the other arm. With your back still straight, bend your knees, leaning your legs back and twisting from side to side, working the centre at the base of the spine. There is a lot of energy in that place: sexual—fighting—joy. If you fall, tuck in your chin and go into a forward roll.

He forward-rolled out of the headstand and was immediately on his feet: 'Now, you begin.'

We began our headstands, struggling against gravity and, in my case, a fear of being upside down. While I was in the headstand, legs leaning back, twisting my lower body, I didn't feel any release of the joyous energy Cynkutis described. I was, quite simply, afraid of falling and

---

1 Illustrations used here and in subsequent chapters were drawn by Bill Ireland under the direction of Cynkutis. For Cynkutis' additional exercises complemented by drawings of vectors and energies, see 'Conversations with the Body' (Cynkutis 2015a: 98–153).

FIGURE 4

injuring my neck. I felt as though I needed training in order to train! Still, like the others, I struggled onward. Cynkutis encouraged us: 'This work increases the body's range. The farther you go the less difficult other things will become.'

He then gave us three more exercises: the backward roll, forward roll, and shoulder stand (a traditional yoga asana). We were instructed to move across the floor by alternating between each of them. Cynkutis counselled us to keep our movements flowing and continuous in order to avoid lapsing into thought and hesitation.

The work was difficult and challenged me at a level I really couldn't meet. Certainly, I could try to 'encounter myself' but that encounter seemed to be mostly a feeling of being inadequate and lost. I had read descriptions of Laboratory Theatre training, including gymnastics, in *Towards a Poor Theatre*. However, experiencing even a small portion of their intensive exercises made me realize the immense dedication required to achieve their level of mastery.

## Vectors in the Body

Cynkutis had brought work with vectors to the Laboratory Theatre; for him, they were an extremely important tool.[2] He spent the rest of the day helping us understand vectors in our bodies.

Cynkutis directed us over to a long, metal railing that protected the stairwell: 'Today we will work again with vectors in the body. You will use this railing to push against and, at the same time, to pull.' He demonstrated how he wanted us to push with one hand while pulling with the other. 'Feel what it is in the middle of your body that allows you to push and pull at the same time. Where is the meeting place of these two vectors?' he asked.

As we worked on the exercise, I felt an area in the core of my body, just below the diaphragm, that was not only engaged but aching from this effort to simultaneously push and pull. After some time, Cynkutis continued: 'Now, without using this railing, I want you to recreate what you have learned. Bring those vectors alive.'

---

2 In a phone interview with me, Richard Mennen said:

> Zbyszek brought the work on vectors, opposing forces, to the Laboratory Theatre. He learnt it from an older teacher at the Łódź film school where he had originally trained. He brought it and enlarged it, amplifying and changing it. He really enabled it. It's easier to grasp work with vectors when it's about posture and gesture. You can see it in dance. Zbyszek also talked about the vectors you can see in works of art. Light and shadow are vectors.
>
> In the afterword to Thomas Richards' book *At Work with Grotowski on Physical Actions* (1995), Grotowski talks about the special work he did with [Ryszard] Cieślak helping him to find the inner life of the Constant Prince. It was an example of a director using a person's personal experience-not in an autobiographical or confessional way-but as another vector that was informing and giving life underneath what was taking place in the performance. The performance then connected to the physical work; to the action, to the movement. When you work with vectors that can't be prescribed. It has to be intimated. You have to get to it through your own action. An action that in a way is less than fully conscious. (Mennen 2020)

Working without the support of the rail took a great deal of concentration and focus, and I immediately became aware that I didn't have good body memory at all. 'If you need to remind your body, you can return again to the railing,' Cynkutis instructed. We continued working for another half hour before he introduced another approach.

'Now you will use the wall, pushing against it and creating within your own body this opposing vector of pulling,' he directed. We struggled to achieve the dynamic tension of the two vectors. But, again, when we moved away from the wall, it was extremely difficult to recreate this.

The work was very demanding and with the oppressive heat of the day we were soon in a sweat and heavy with exhaustion. Cynkutis gave us an image to encourage the work: 'Imagine what energy you will need to pull a horse out of a saloon! You will need to push strongly with one part of your body so that you can pull with the other to get this horse!' Extending his arms as though holding onto the imaginary reins of the horse, he made sure we understood the vectors involved: 'Your chest is pulled in the direction of the horse and your hips are pushing in the opposite direction. Keep arms loose and hands relaxed.'

FIGURE 5

We threw ourselves back into the work with enthusiasm, our imaginations inspired by this Wild West fantasy. Without letting our momentum drop, Cynkutis moved us on to another task: 'Now imagine that there is a wall in front of you. Place your hands flat against this imaginary wall. Your chest is pushing towards this wall and your leg is pushing against the floor creating an opposite vector. Your hands are stable and do not move, signalling to the audience this symbol: "wall".'

By now, I was becoming very discouraged as the work continued to prove difficult for me. I couldn't seem to find the vectors in my body that would create this imaginary wall. Fortunately, Cynkutis didn't leave any time between exercises for reflection; he immediately moved us on to the next challenge:

> Find a partner, face them, and clasp each other's hands. Push your partner's hand with one hand and pull their other hand with your other hand. Your partner works with you, pushing with the hand that you are pushing with and pulling with the hand that you are pulling with. Your legs are free to move and dance around this centre, but this energy in the middle between you and your partner is constant.

Elizabeth made no movement to join in. She flopped down on the floor, her face red from effort, 'What does any of this have to do with acting in a play?' she demanded.

Cynkutis paused, letting the moment sink in, before responding:

> Well, Elizabeth, it is really quite simple. Vectors can be used quite practically to create physical tensions that might be necessary in a scene. For example, in Shakespeare's play *Othello*, there is the moment when the pillow is put upon the face of Desdemona and her breath is stopped. By using opposing vectors and working together, the actors who play Othello and Desdemona can create this struggle between them, creating real tension while not endangering anyone. Or, if called upon to prepare a scene in which there is a fight, the actors can use vectors for the necessary tensions, together or singly, moment to moment. Vectors bring a strong and immediate connection to the partner. For individual actors, using vectors creates an alive body, one that is not

> collapsed and without vitality. Vectors bring presence. Even when you are sitting still on the stage, if vectors are engaged there is real life in the body.

With that answer, we continued our work.

At first, I was relieved to be working with a partner, but it soon became clear that now I couldn't disengage even when I was tired. With gripped hands and sweaty palms, we danced around each other, unable to let loose even for a moment. Soon enough, though, Cynkutis began choosing people to work one-on-one with him, allowing the rest of us to watch. Through observation, it became very clear when the force created by opposing vectors was truly present and when it was not. When Cynkutis partnered with Judith, I could clearly see this invisible connection with the partner, existing like a third force in the space between them.

After the training session, I stayed behind to speak with Cynkutis because during the earlier push/pull exercises, I had experienced a dull pain in my stomach area that made me feel like crying. He had me perform the exercise again at the railing while watching me closely and said:

> You are feeling this way because the centre you are using to perform this exercise, the area of the diaphragm, is probably irritated and it is not the right centre anyway. The centre you should be using is at the *base* of the spinal column and extends upward through the arms. Perhaps it is a problem with your construction that you are touching a nerve centre associated with crying. Try to focus on having the source for this exercise come from the base of your spine.

Back at my dorm room, I lay down for a short rest before the upcoming evening session and fell into a dream.

### Journal entry, afternoon of 18 June 1984

*I dreamed that I asked Zbyszek, 'What can we do when this is over and we have no one to work with, no good director?' He said, 'Not everyone has such shallow ideals.' I think what the dream meant was—find deeper people to work with, no matter what their position is. In the dream, I also asked him about inspiration and how to find the meaning in a piece. He told me to look at what was going on in my life. To take from life what moved me, what I wished to explore, and what I questioned. Strange, it was all a dream, yet it felt exactly like we had a conversation.*

CHAPTER SEVEN

# THE TRINITY: BODY, VOICE, AND IMAGE

## Monday, 18 June 1984: Evening Session in the Theatre

> *Body, voice, and imagination are together. When two of these are present, when two of these are fully engaged,* [ . . . ] *the other one comes and makes a certain whole.*

The evening began with a continuation of our work with partners.

### Partner Work / Vectors

Cynkutis described the task: 'Imagine that there is a balloon between your body and the body of your partner. When your partner pushes towards you, you feel the pressure from this balloon and your body responds. When you press forward, your partner also responds to this balloon. Try to create this reality.'

Judith was my partner, always a dynamic experience. Somehow, we had to establish the reality of this balloon between us. I wanted to begin slowly, but Judith began strong movements towards me, and I had to respond with equal energy. Soon we were fully concentrated on the give-and-take. Occasionally I felt a subtle, energetic bond with Judith when our concentration was so focused that for a few moments this imaginary balloon really did exist. The creation of this third reality between us became the goal.

This task reminded me of the theatre exercise 'Mirrors', where the objective is to mirror a partner's movements so closely that it is unclear, even to those doing the exercise, who leads and who follows. Though similar, the 'Balloon' exercise connected me much more viscerally with my partner. Instead of some kind of vague slow-motion merging, I needed to be immediately responsive to my partner's actions. It was a good, visceral approach for a theatre in which tensions and exchanges between partners were dynamic and real.

Cynkutis walked among us, coaching us, adding additional images to explore: 'Now, what is between you and your partner is an elastic band; later, it will become a rope.'

As we drew from these different images, small, story-like vignettes arose. They were a constant surprise and a satisfying element of the exercises. In my work with Judith, there were times when, due to our configuration and the strength of her force, it seemed that I was ruled over by a domineering mother. I knew from experience that if these associations were strong enough and shed light on the theme of a piece, they could be built upon and used in a production. Because of their organic base, these moments would not just be empty representations of an idea that a director or advisor had; they would be grounded in the actor's bodies and in how they sensed each other.

## Creating Environments with Body and Image

Without giving us time to relax, Cynkutis moved us into an exploration of our environment, saying: 'Now you are no longer focused on your partner, but on the environment that you are in. Everything here is covered with honey. How can you move in this honey? Use the plastiques to keep your body alive.'

The way Cynkutis said the word 'honey' slowed us down. Not only his words, but the sound and quality of his voice seemed designed to lead us into the experience.

'Now, your environment: the chairs, the wooden boxes, everything here is covered in fur. Improvise with this association. Explore it with your body,' he continued.

After we had explored that image Cynkutis said, 'Work only with the hips. Keeping pelvic rotations alive, concentrate your attention in the area of your sex. Your sex is a bell and it is ringing.' Giving us time to work with each subsequent image, he called out, 'Your sex is a kitten exploring the space. Now, it is a knife! Now, your sex is a hole with the wind whistling through it.' One by one we explored the images. It was unusual to be asked to experience anything in this area of the body. I felt like I was jumping over inner restrictions to encounter it at all. But the playfulness and diversity of the images challenged us to be present and to be engaged with this undiscovered territory at the base of the spine.

Cynkutis then opened up the exploration to whatever would arise for us: 'Discover in your own way. Keep this area alive.' We continued our work, seeing what images would appear, but as we tried to explore on our own, the task became uncomfortable. I became much more aware of the others in the space. Was this an invasion of our privacy or a way of having us engage parts of ourselves usually kept off limits? At the end of the exercise, Cynkutis directly addressed the awkwardness of the group. His tone was quiet but certain as he explained to us why we should engage all aspects of ourselves in the work:

## Conversation: Disciplining Sexual Energy

> In theatre, we have to be able to work with all parts of ourselves and not to say that this or that is bad or 'dirty'. Sex is a very important source of energy for theatre and we must know how to work with it and also how to discipline it. The way to discipline it is with associations. It must not be worked with directly, with personal emotions, exposing yourself. If you are working with a partner, transform your partner into something else. 'My fingers through his hair is like touching the meadow grass,' 'I am caressing her arm like a river in a riverbed,' 'She is a palm and I am the wind which bends the palm.' The energy must be translated to

protect the actors and also to free the actors. But it needs to be available for the stage or a great deal of power and an important part of ourselves will not be available for the work.[1]

In art, sex can be approached also in a very religious way.

'Religious?' Elizabeth had shock and surprise in her voice.

Certainly. I remember there were a few times I saw, in works of art, two people in this 'act of love'—I prefer 'act of love' to 'making love' because it should not be mechanical—and this act of love was very religious.

One time was when I saw a painter who was doing paintings of people preparing for the journey to this act of love. It was unbelievable how it was depicted. From step to step, they were closer and closer, and at the last picture they made love. But it was like the last way of Christ from station to station. Can you imagine? Like in church you have these pictures—stations of the cross—his last way before he was crucified.

'Is that how it felt?' Judith asked.

Yeah, it was very painful and very beautiful. Incredible. It is strange what it can mean, 'the last way of Christ'. Unbelievable,

---

1 Cynkutis reflects on the importance of having the erotic or sexual energy of the actor available when he writes in his personal 'Notebook-Diary' on the development of his role as the title character in *Faustus*:

> Grot himself, and here I fully agree with him, justifies the use of [erotic] associations in artistic work by saying that this is the domain of the actor's strongest sensations, through which the creative process can be liberated and through which a score of actions—where the composition of signs will in the end not resemble an erotic situation at all—can subsequently be established. However, carried by an erotic impulse, this will appeal to the spectator's own associations related to this area, and, beyond all rationality, stir in them images, feelings, and very intimate psychic states. At this moment the essence of the performance will come into being: that is, a spark jumping between the actor and the spectator. (2015b: 76)

how he touched the girl and how they cooperated together. These artistic pictures were full of very religious things.

Cynkutis then spoke about the role of theatre in society:

## Conversation: Food for the Spirit

[Audio #4] The idea of theatre at the beginning was not to show people something like stories, but to provide people with food for their spirit, food for feelings, food for this life which we have inside of us. To create a certain togetherness among the human species which organically doesn't exist.

The very first theatre, probably, was something that took care of how this group of people, living near one another, how among these people, even for a short time, a feeling of togetherness can be created. And it was sure that this togetherness can happen only when all of these people will be involved in something that for all of them is the same: how to join people through a certain feeling, through a certain spiritual state, through a certain emotional state. That's why, for instance, sports today is social . . . that's why theatre. A great amount of people, in one place at one time, are able to forget about everything else to focus totally on the activity which can stimulate among them energy.

This is, more or less, the idea of acting. People are coming and our idea is to stimulate among them such an energy that can help them forget, for a moment, about how everyone hates or doesn't like someone who is standing in front of them. A moment in which we all can feel close, spiritually close, accepting differences, tolerating differences, but together. Do you understand what I mean? This is a great psychological idea.

Theatre has a very strong psychological function and a very strong educational function. But education doesn't mean to make lessons and to say what is good and what is not good, what

> is black and what is white, what is nasty and what is wonderful. That is not education. This didactic approach is naïve and certainly it is wrong. Pedagogy means to help people to understand the world in which we are living, with all the differences that are in the world. Not to try to make a uniform world and to make that this is wrong and this is right. It is right and wrong at the same time. It is good and bad at the same time, and it must be like that. And even if it is bad, it is not a reason to kill someone. And even if is good, it is not a case to glorify someone, to make them a star or hero, because that is exactly what makes divisions and fights. **[End Audio #4]**

The conversation over, we gathered on the stage as he presented the next task:

## The Voice as a Presence

'The voice is a real presence existing in the space. Can you imagine? You can put your voice in different places in the environment.' He demonstrated: 'My voice is on the ceiling . . . My voice is climbing up the wall . . . My voice is in the shadow.' His voice seemed to emanate from the different areas he named. 'So—to the task—put your voice in different places. You can think also that your voice comes from there.'

After we had worked in this way for a long time, Cynkutis introduced another element:

'The voice can also have an association and an intention, for example, a spider making its web.' Cynkutis began speaking a text in Polish. His voice started softly and grew in power, a tangible presence that unrolled like a thick web across the theatre extending into the audience area, spanning the space. I felt it as a palpable force, spreading out with a kind of dark energy from where he stood. Never had I imagined that the voice could be such a real physical presence. I was stunned by the demonstration.

Cynkutis focused us back on our own work: 'Now, explore the space with your voice. Find where your voice can hide and from where it can make an attack. Work also with your echo. Do things to the space with your voice, investigate and find what the response will be.'

Inspired by his example, our efforts had a new intensity. We had just witnessed something we never imagined was possible. We searched with our voices to find the hidden possibilities of the space, finding velvety, resonant pockets for our voices to nestle in and experiencing the sharp ricochets when our attacking voices were repelled by metallic surfaces. After we had explored for almost an hour, Cynkutis introduced a new source for our work:

## Sourcing Animals (I)

> In this next task, I want you to use as a source an animal which I will name for you. See the animal. Let your body become the body of this animal. Take time. Try to remember and to have this animal in your body precisely. Find the animal in your body. Not only *what* it does physically, but *why* it does it.[2]

---

2 Kermit Dunkelberg interviewed director, writer, and actor-training specialist Kim Mancuso for his PhD dissertation titled 'Grotowski and North American Theatre: Translation, Transmission, Dissemination' (2008). Mancuso, who eventually served as director of the International Company of Actors at Second Studio in Wrocław, says:

> [Working with animal associations] was very new for me, but it seemed very logical—to kind of build a character, and when I say 'character', I don't mean in a Stanislavskian sense, but to build a physical structure out of which to express something new, based on the structure of an animal [ . . . ]. [Cynkutis] would call out the name of an animal, and we would have to find the most clichéd posture of that animal that we could. I remember too, we [ . . . ] included [ . . . ] the way we thought these animals might sound. Then he would have us freeze, and we would have to adjust our spines, and adjust the way we moved our heads, and adjust the way

One by one we explored the different animals Cynkutis named: hen, rabbit, camel, goat, and bear. After we had been working quite a long time with 'bear', Cynkutis saw something he wanted to pursue, 'Keeping what you have found, your bear now becomes a beggar by the side of the road.'

Without lapsing back into our usual postures, we brought our physicality of bear straight into the improvisation, lumbering over into a loose line that became our 'side of the road'. Some stood, some sat in heavy poses. The specificity of what we had found kept our entry into the improvisation grounded.

The slow, paw-like movement of my hands and the sensation of thick, heavy nails I'd been exploring as my bear-character brought an association of a beggar from Dickensian England with hands wrapped in thick rags, swollen from alcohol abuse. With that as a strong image to hold on to, I began to explore the situation of a beggar by the side of the road. Aware of my awkward proximity to the others and of their similar need for alms, I was soon jostling them for a better space for the begging. It all felt so natural. My desire to compete came from impulses rooted in my physicality and the given situation not from any concept that I thought up or from something imposed by a director.

I'd improvised with animal characters in traditional theatre programmes in the past, but in those cases the casualness of the approach and the speed with which results were found led to superficial results. Cynkutis' request to find the specificity and reason behind every movement, along with the gravity of his approach, focused the work. His strong

---

we worked with our eyes. He had us thinking about the way different animals looked at the world. We'd do that for a while, and then we'd freeze again, and memorize the structure in the spine, and then continue to work as the animal, meaning moving around the space [ . . . ]. [W]e would relate to the other animals. Then he would propose different settings for these animals. So, a horse lying down in a field at night, or a horse drinking from a cold stream, or a horse on ice, or a horse running down a forest path [ . . . ]. (In Dunkelberg 2008: 534–35)

watchful presence let us know that there was something very important to discover here.

Cynkutis then requested that we use a vulture as a source for our character. After initial work with the bird's body and movements, he suggested that our vulture was a pilgrim. Character impulses emerged from this work as well.[3]

Cynkutis now focused his attention on something he had observed earlier: 'I want to return, Diane, to your work with rabbit. Repeat, please, what you did before but keep your text from *Long Day's Journey into Night* nearby. There may be a moment in which it will be useful.'

I went back to my work with rabbit, first visualizing it and then taking its body image as my own, which stimulated a variety of organic adjustments. I began making the different movements I had seen rabbits do, for instance: cleaning the ears with the paws. I used my right hand to stroke my 'ears' from the back of my neck up and over my head. As I did that motion, my head twisted down and to the side. Cynkutis saw something in these movements and asked me to continue to repeat them: 'Keeping your work, not losing that source, bring your rabbit over to the chair and sit on the chair as this rabbit. You can even let go of the movement and stay with this feeling, the sensation you have discovered in your neck.'

---

3 The following quote from Cynkutis is from notes taken by David Russell, an acting student who participated in Cynkutis' 1983 workshop at Smith College:

> If you are playing a role, for instance, Hamlet, the interesting thing is not to be, for instance, Zbyszek on stage playing Hamlet. Zbyszek on stage is boring! Imagine what animal the character, Hamlet, reminds you of. For me it is a vulture. Then find how this animal moves, calls, what leads its body. Taking one or two secret points from your exploration, make them smaller, put them into human form and movement. Hide them in humanness but leave them as physical and vocal impulses and motivation. (Russell 1983: 1)

The motion I was making had created an energetic feeling along the right side of my neck, combined with a kind of tightness. While keeping all my focus on that physical and energetic source, I made my way over to one of the wooden chairs and perched lightly on it. Cynkutis continued:

> From this place in your neck where you feel the impulse of rabbit, from that source, bring us the voice of this rabbit. Do not make an idea of this voice. Hold your image and your body for 'rabbit' and let the voice come from there. You will not even know what voice will come and it does not matter what you say. It can even be counting.

I held on to the sensation, and as I began to count, a voice emerged. It skipped along, high and tremulous. It was absolutely right for rabbit. Because I hadn't preconceived it, my voice was free and light. I was allowing it rather than controlling it. I continued counting and the numbers pattered on as I held onto my sources: the image of rabbit and the body adjustments that had led to the energetic sensation along the side and back of my neck.

Cynkutis guided the process: 'Keeping the place in your body you have found, find the walk of this rabbit. The counting also can continue.'

A scampering, little walk developed, but I had to be careful to maintain contact with my sources, otherwise I could feel the solidity of my work disintegrate. I had to keep returning to my image of rabbit and the sensation in my neck.

'Thank you, Diane, you may sit down.' Cynkutis turned to the group, 'So from this starting point of rabbit, from the body and this picture of rabbit, a voice came that even she did not expect. Is that right, Diane?'

'Yes.'

> She was able to let it come—and it will come—and this is why; it is something like a principle. If you have two vectors—in this case the first vector was 'image of this rabbit', and the second vector, 'body of this rabbit'—then a third element, voice, will come. This

> third element will come if we are not creating an idea, if we are not in the way. Body, voice, and imagination are together. When two of these are present, when two of these are fully engaged, truthfully engaged, the other one comes and makes a certain whole.

Judith asked, 'Does it always happen the same, that from an image and the body comes the voice?' Cynkutis responded:

> That is one way, but it is also true that if you have the picture of rabbit in your imagination and through it you have found the voice, you will see that your body will be moved and create the third point of, let's say, of this triangle. It can also be that if you sense your voice and body are together creating something strong, you can find that slowly the image will come that is informing them. It depends on the task and it depends upon the construction of each actor. So, when Diane moved slowly onto the chair, not rushing the task, careful not to lose connection to this source in nature that she had found, that was the right approach. She continued with work, letting the voice arise using the text—in this example counting but it could be anything to begin—and she was able to go off on her own, still drinking from this source. Not so much to express 'what is rabbit', but to express what was feeding her from this image. Do you understand?

We nodded in affirmation.

'Thank you everyone. We will meet again tomorrow,' Cynkutis concluded.

I stepped out of the theatre into the soft, summer night feeling as though I was walking on air. It was a feeling of euphoria I wished could last forever.

### Journal entry, evening of 18 June 1984

*Today was just an incredible day. I can't believe how liberating it is to find a character or a voice through sourcing it in this way. It's a totally new experience for me. It reminds me of a story I heard about Lawrence Olivier. Supposedly he was waiting for his entrance and, just before it, he tensed a calf muscle and his whole character came to life. Perhaps that was his physical source and, like the work today, it was found in a muscular configuration—although we engaged much more than just the body. What Zbyszek is speaking of, working with Body, Voice, and Imagination as though two of them can call forth the third is an amazing tool.*

CHAPTER EIGHT

# TRAINING WITH OBJECTS AND VECTORS

## Tuesday, 19 June 1984: Daytime Session in the Theatre

> *You can believe what you are doing because there is something in your body that is leading you. You are not pretending. You are taking care of something.*

As usual, our sessions began with individual warm-ups. The plastiques were always an important focus as their purpose was to open up the whole body. Today, Cynkutis coached us in this opening work, leading us into immediate action.

'Using the plastiques, move and stir the energy in the space,' he began. We took off around the room rotating and spinning, increasing whatever energy was there with the energy we were creating. He continued to urge us on: 'Now, everything you encounter, an object, a person, whatever you see, take its vectors into your body. Experience this exchange fully and then move quickly to the next. Use small elements from the rotations to keep your whole body alive.' We followed his instructions and as we continued, he increased the pace till we were almost running. Working till we were almost at the point of collapse.

### The Spine and Life of a Prop

After giving us time to rest and write in our journals, Cynkutis focused us on a new task:

> I want you to explore an object, a prop, one that is medium to large in size. Choose your object and come near to it. With your body, take on its planes and surfaces—even the textures of the

surfaces can become a part of you. In your body, find the vectors which are the spine and the life of this object.

I chose a chair as my object and as I worked, taking its planes and vectors into my body, I began to feel something like a magnetic pull developing between myself and the chair.

Cynkutis continued developing our work: 'Wrap yourself like a snake around this prop. Can you carry it with no hands and without manipulating it? Maybe this object even has a life of its own.' I was around and under the chair now, entangled as I attempted to lift and carry it.

'When I call "Stop!" see what associations and images arise from how your body *is* in relation to the object. Explore any image that comes. If you find you are trapped in thinking, use the plastiques to gently bring you back to the body; to keep your body alive,' Cynkutis directed.

After a long time in which Cynkutis called out 'Stop!' and we explored, he instructed us to continue working without stopping: 'Take time, explore with the body. Discover what images, what story is created by how your body meets this object.'

The work felt rich and full. I was completely absorbed by the images that arose from this spontaneous work in relation to an object.[1]

---

1 The use of objects in Grotowski's 'poor theatre' was revolutionary. Interaction with props was a dynamic part of the creation of every piece. According to Ludwik Flaszen:

> There are no 'sets' in the usual sense of the word. They have been reduced to the objects which are indispensable to the dramatic action. Each object must contribute not to the meaning but to the dynamics of the play; its value resides in its various uses [ . . . ] as a concrete three-dimensional metaphor which contributes to the creation of the vision. [ . . . ] Each object has multiple uses. The bathtub is a very pedestrian bathtub; on the other hand [in *Akropolis*] it is a symbolical bathtub: it represents all the bathtubs in which human bodies were processed for the making of soap and leather. Turned upside down, the same bathtub becomes an altar in front of which an inmate chants a prayer. Set up in a high place, it becomes Jacob's nuptial bed. (In Grotowski 1968: 75–76).

## Work with Balance

Cynkutis then introduced a completely different approach to work with an object:

> Take some kind of heavy object and hold it in front of you. Find the point at which its weight tips you forward. Then hold the object close to you and find the point where it seems that you are holding no weight at all. Find where the object forces you to lean or not to lean. Explore this in different directions.

Although this seemed a simple exercise, finer levels of physical awareness were always possible. As different muscles adjusted to the weight, I tried to sensitize myself to each change in my body. Cynkutis then challenged our physical memory: 'Put your object away and continue to explore as though you were still holding it. Move through the space. How do you sit while carrying this weight?'

It was difficult to get my body to respond fully to this remembered situation. I had to keep commanding it to be active, consciously engaging my muscles and reminding myself again and again how my body had been leaning and what opposing force had held it there. After we had explored the exercise for a long time, Cynkutis gave an example of how physical tasks truthfully executed create authenticity for both actor and audience.

## Vectors: Old Age and Youth

'Imagine you have been asked to play an old person and you have put five pounds of make-up on your face,' Cynkutis said, his eyes full of fun as he conjured the situation. 'If you do not do something else that will help you to believe that you are older, you will never feel comfortable and it will bother you.'

He continued to explain his approach:

> Even for young actors, it is a possibility to play an old person if you find out how to understand the problem of the body. Not

how to indicate, but how to understand. One search can be done with everything that limits your balance, because among old people there is something in common—this limit. The reasons for this are different—someone has pain in the spinal cord, someone has pain in the feet or the knees—but this pain speaks to this elderly person and says, 'Don't do that! Don't move like that! Don't change your rhythms! Don't turn!' It is like the pain is saying what to do and what not to do.

By lifting something, you will really feel where this limit is placed and from this comes a certain step, certain ways of changing directions and sitting and knowledge how to protect the body. So you will never kneel down like before, but rather you will search how to kneel down. You can still do it, but it is very different. And this awareness—this feeling which is leading your body to work in this way—leads also to a certain character. You can believe what you are doing because there is something in your body that is leading you. You are not pretending. You are taking care of something. So it is quite an easy way. After several hours of rehearsing, you can find a very powerful tool. Even if your movement will not be made completely realistically, after a few minutes, people watching feel that you do understand certain things, and they believe.

And you can spend several evenings taking lighter or heavier things and trying always to search, not how easily you can do this, but where is the moment in which the object lifted by you has an effect on your spine. Because old age, starts in the spinal column. It is the secret of being old. The spine is getting more and more tense and the body moves less easily. When the body moves less, everything is getting more stuck and later the brain is getting stuck! But everything starts from the spine.

Another approach to portraying old age is by using an image. For instance, one element of old age is the release of a kind of

> sexual winter. It is as if this place, which when we are young we associate with a hot spot, in old age is neutral or cold. A possible image to work with is that the area of sex is cold or wounded. If it works for you, you will imagine it, and that image will affect your whole body and how it is held.
>
> Today, we will explore old age using vectors. This initiates a problem that is connected with balance. Please take into your hands something that is not very heavy but heavy enough and hold it in front of your body.

We began choosing our objects. Judith picked up a plastic pitcher that was nearby. Cynkutis immediately responded:

> Not at all, Judith, that is too light. Choose something that has five or more pounds. Yes, a chair is OK. Keep it close to your body. What you have is too light, Elizabeth, it is too light. Perhaps we should all work then with chairs . . . .
>
> Hold the chair away from your body to find a way that it changes your spine. Try different positions until you find one that is interesting. The vector of your body opposes the vector of the chair and creates this lean, this limit. Keep this dynamic in the body until you can work without the chair. Develop the walk of your character using the vectors that you find.

Holding the chair in various positions affected our walk and all of our movements. Cynkutis then asked us to face the back of the chair: 'Put your hands on the back of the chair and push down on it with one hand. While still pushing with that hand and keeping that vector, create an opposing vector trying to pull the chair up into the air with the other hand.' He demonstrated as he spoke.

After we had worked in this way for half an hour, he followed up with another exploration:

> For someone who is old, the vector is more down, whereas in youth, there is more energy to rise, to go up. Stay seated in your

chair and engage the two vectors of rising and falling within your body. When the inner motion up is stronger, that is the more youthful body's energy rising up. When the inner motion is stronger down, that is the body when it is old.

We tried the exercise and I was amazed at how different the experience of my body was depending on which vector was stronger.

'Even if you don't plan on playing different characters, you can still research how many different ways you can carry your body. You can, for instance, hold a chair on your right side.' He demonstrated, holding a chair off the ground in his right hand. 'You ask your body, "How will you balance?"' Cynkutis' body configuration changed because of its relationship to the weight of the chair. 'Only because of this chair do I arrive at this certain way of balancing. Do you remember this movement by Monty Python actors?' Cynkutis demonstrated an unusual and very funny walk that had us all laughing.

It was incredible—the competition among them for the funniest steps. It was called 'The Ministry of Silly Walks'. The actors who made this comedy investigated new possibilities for the body by just such a play with balance. Have you seen films with Jacques Tati, like *Mr Hulot's Holiday* [1953], in which he was walking all the time as though he was falling down? Unbelievable possibilities found in the actor's movement and such fun. I watched this a few times, and I had such a pain in my stomach from laughing. When I saw this man who was walking all the time almost like . . . .

[*He begins to demonstrate.*]

I cannot do it, but I can imagine that I can train to do it. He developed this walk with training. He found that with objects, with something in his hand, he was able to find such a position and he trained how to walk in this position.

### Scene Improvisation Using Vectors

'So, just as those actors did, let us use our work with vectors as a tool for improvisation! Jackie, come here please.' Cynkutis pulled a table and chair into the middle of the space. 'You are a clerk and this table is your desk. Arrange your office for a meeting. Relate to each chair before moving it. Use the opposing vectors of pushing and pulling to keep an active body while lifting and placing each chair.'

Jackie had good physical control and her intense involvement in what she was doing gave her a strong presence. But when she had finished arranging the chairs and sat behind the desk, the energy in her body visibly dissipated.

'Do not lose your presence while in the chair; keep the vectors of rising and falling from the previous exercise active in your body even when you are still,' Cynkutis coached.

Jackie gave the work with vectors her full focus and commitment. Summoning the opposing tensions, her presence was again alive and full. Cynkutis turned to the rest of us:

> Each of you now may enter this office Jackie has made. In this improvisation, the energy will go to the person who speaks the most important text. Find out who this person is and engage with this person using one vector towards and another away. The leader must create chains that unite all the others to them. Discover who is the leader!

My body immediately tensed as if for battle. Which chair should I take to position myself to lead? I plotted to take over Jackie's chair. It was in a strategic position behind the barricade of the desk which had already been established as a seat of control and power.

As we entered the space the fight for supremacy began with the shouting of texts, intensity of sound and elongated words. It was a tumultuous scene with no clear winner until Jackie left her seat and came in front of the desk to challenge everyone. I swept behind her, jumped onto her chair and then leapt onto the desk. All focus turned to me as I struggled, wolf-like, to keep my dominance using body and text. As we continued to move and struggle, trading texts, searching for active vectors in our bodies that could keep us both towards and against each other, I tried to create the imaginary energetic chains that would tie the group to me. In all probability it was more chaos than anything else but we were all energized and activated by the task.

When the improvisation had reached a natural end, Cynkutis closed our morning session with an assignment: 'Yesterday, we began our work with animals as the source of a character. Before our evening session, find a creature which for you associates with your role in *Long Day's Journey into Night*.'

As I traversed the campus wondering what animal to associate with Mary Tyrone, I saw a salamander dart down into a culvert. Its movements were quicksilver and energetic. I caught it and it flipped over in my hand, its soft belly facing up, helplessly wriggling. This would be my choice for Mary. She was like this creature in her slippery, desperate avoidance of reality and deep-rooted vulnerability.

CHAPTER NINE

# TRANSFORMATIONS

## Tuesday, 19 June 1984: Evening Session in the Theatre

*The object is never just what it is; it also is a vehicle for expression.*

### Sourcing Animals (II)

Cynkutis gathered us onto the stage to begin:

> This evening, we will start by working with the animal you have chosen. In this stage environment, find the place where your animal wants to be, where it wants to hide or whatever it is. Take time. Take time. When you have found a place that feels right, begin exploring the body and movement of your animal.

Similar to how we searched for the right place for our tree, finding the right spot for our animal rooted us in intuitive awareness. Instinctively, my sense of salamander drew me to dark, hidden places. The shadowy space near the legs of a large chair and the base of the backstage curtain felt right. I decided to use both of them.

Cynkutis continued to coach us:

> After you have found the body of your animal, explore what your animal is doing. Be specific and be present in the space. If your action in this moment leads to sound, then let the voice of this animal come. It does not matter what you say. Do not worry about the words or the sense of the text. If it is right, meaning will come. You do not have to make it.

I focused on my memory of the salamander, its wiry spine and tense, muscular body. As I took the image and tensions into my body, I felt a subcutaneous shimmering that radiated energy from my spine down into my hands. Holding onto this feeling as a source, I began to count. The numbers spilt out quickly as a high voice emerged. Adding the element of voice had suddenly released me into a full-blown experience of being the salamander trying to escape. It overcame me in spurts, causing me to dart back and forth from the back curtains to the base of the chair. This was not at all a realistic expression of a character, but Cynkutis' continual emphasis on commitment to the task led me not to care whether or not it was naturalistic or how it would look to others. Certainly he wanted us to go as far as possible, to take our imaginings absolutely seriously. How else could it be a real risk?

The work took every bit of concentration I had. Even still, I had difficulty sustaining my salamander character beyond those bursts of frenetic energy. After almost an hour, Cynkutis added the next element to our explorations:

> In the next task, you will use your text from *Long Day's Journey into Night*. I asked you to choose this text but not memorize it. We are working and we do not want to fix it. Find the way your animal will sit on a chair and say the text. Use the text as sounds just as we have used numbers or letters. It can even be one sentence you will use and repeat. You may pick up your paper in a moment or put it down, it does not matter. What matters is your concentration on the task. Elizabeth and Jackie, your text is part of a scene together but, for now, I want you to work separately as you explore your text and your animal.

This task, with its use of realistic text and the human act of sitting on a chair, seemed a difficult stretch from where I was right now with my creature. I was concerned that I would lose all the work I'd done before. I decided to stay with the physicality I'd found and coax myself onto the seat of the chair before trying to say the words of the text.

After several attempts in which I failed to get there or even convince myself that this was the right place to be, I squirmed onto the chair like a reluctant witness at a trial. Uneasy at being so conspicuous and gripping my text with a shaking hand, I found a sentence and began to speak. I ignored the meaning of the words and worked with sound, repeating my text over and over. My phrasing and pauses echoed my creature's discomfort while the sense of being on trial provided insight into the character of Mary Tyrone who feels, quite rightly, that she is being watched. The exploration was raw and rough but because I was committed to my animal image, it felt honest. Throughout the process, new meanings and new experiences emerged.

'Everyone come and sit to the side except for Elizabeth and Jackie who will work on their scene,' said Cynkutis. 'Mary is alone in the house with Cathleen, her servant. With these boxes or chairs please make the place where you meet.'

Elizabeth and Jackie dragged one of our few pieces of real furniture, a soft divan, across the back of the space.

'Take the individual work you have done into this exchange between Mary and Cathleen,' Cynkutis directed.

The scene played out fairly naturalistically with Elizabeth seated on the divan as Mary Tyrone and Jackie as the household servant, Cathleen, hovering near her. But they seemed to be focusing only on creating a normal human exchange. After this initial attempt, Cynkutis asked them to ground themselves more strongly in their animal associations. This time, Jackie was more energized, almost predatory, and that in turn stimulated Elizabeth to shrink from her. The resulting relationship seemed to surprise even the actors themselves.

'OK, this is already a beginning, but it is not very fully realized. Take time to focus again on your animal. Stay with its body and voice as you begin again the scene,' Cynkutis coached.

This time, Jackie gave herself over completely to her animal association, hovering hungrily around Elizabeth. It was clear that her animal was a predator. But Elizabeth was having trouble and seemed unable to channel her emotions into the scene. She was clearly not enjoying the focus on their work and suddenly broke away from Jackie saying, 'I can't do this anymore! I'm tired and I didn't even get any sleep last night!' She started crying, and then added, with accusation in her voice, 'All this work is really hard, and you never give us any breaks!'

'It is important to continue, Elizabeth, and not let this moment stop you,' Cynkutis gently cautioned. But Elizabeth only began to sob harder, speaking of how difficult her life was.

'Elizabeth . . . Elizabeth . . . ' Cynkutis repeated her name softly several times to get her attention, 'Elizabeth, please do not continue to speak. I wish to explain something to everyone.'

Cynkutis took several long moments of silence, letting the quiet permeate the room. He spoke slowly, with clarity and compassion, diffusing the charged energy that had been created in the space:

> It is important in this work not to bring our personal life into the space. It is a very easy and a very bad way to ruin not only your own work but also that of others. When we come here, it is not a daily space where we can say whatever we want and bring our personal selves into the picture. When we come to this place where we will conduct our work, our daily self is left at the door. If you must cry, cry, but do not break your work or damage the environment for others. I want to be clear, as this is a most fundamental point. Elizabeth, do you understand?

Elizabeth, head down and face wet with tears, nodded.

'This is important not just for you, but for everyone to know. That is why I am slowly taking this time.'

Cynkutis let the silence settle once more and then switched to a new exercise, gathering several small objects from the props closet and placing them on a table.

### Transforming Objects

He gestured to the props: 'For this exploration of your text, I want you to choose an object from this table or from what you have brought with you today. It is important not to be such a pragmatist that you work with this object with its daily uses. The object is never just what it is; it also is a vehicle for expression.'

We each selected our objects. David and Elizabeth both chose pen and paper. Cynkutis started us off with specific associations: 'David, imagine that this pen you hold is a rifle and the paper is a bullet. Elizabeth your pen is a horse and the paper is a meadow. Diane, for you, the hairbrush you have selected is a bow and your hair is the violin. Your text and the sound of your voice accompanies this work.'

Judith was sitting in the divan with a newspaper open in her lap. Cynkutis went over and began working with her: 'Judith, if you are working with a newspaper with your text: 'I saw dark silence. Dark silence and alarm in my ear,'[1] do not think it is a newspaper. It is a butterfly, or a smelly fish, or mud. Speak the text with this newspaper as if you are speaking through mud or as though you are sinking in mud.'

Cynkutis called us over to watch Judith's work. As she focused on the image, her newspaper became like thick mud that her voice struggled to find a way through bringing a completely different quality to her usual vocal precision. The association also brought insights into her text that would never have been found had the object been treated realistically.

'Now, work without the newspaper and explore what is this "dark silence". Touch by your voice "dark silence",' suggested Cynkutis.

Judith put the newspaper to the side. Her eyes seemed to focus on something far away. As she spoke, an eerie quality permeated her voice. I felt chills run up the back of my spine.

---

1 Judith had been allowed to work with text from a poem instead of text from *Long Day's Journey into Night.*

Cynkutis continued to work with each of us: 'Diane, please change the association for your object. Now the hairbrush becomes a paintbrush and your hair is the canvas. What is the thickness of the paint? What are the colours?'

He guided each of us with questions that led us deeper into our work. The more specific we were, the more invested we became in the association. By not focusing on the literal meaning of the words, our vocal expression was interesting and spontaneous. Cynkutis stood to the side to watch while encouraging us to take the lead:

> I want you to continue exploring with your object, but this time *you* will find the associations to try. It can be totally absurd but if it gives a different depth and different understanding to your text, you may decide to keep it for work later. Explore your prop as if it is something new and with unknown possibilities and see what associations you will find.

We continued until late in the evening. It had been a long and intense session, and when I returned to the dorm room, I collapsed into a chair by the window to write about the experiences of the day.

## Journal entry, evening of 19 June 1984

*This work with animal associations is overwhelming. I don't know how to sustain the energy. It keeps draining away after these bursts. The work with objects was slow in coming but eventually I was better able to transform my body and voice. When it was just a general idea of painting, it was not very strong. But because Zbyszek kept questioning me to be more specific, I was able to concentrate more intently, and my body was involved in interesting ways. I chose to paint my hair as Picasso painted upon a canvas in his Blue Period! NEVER FORGET! If you want to be focused and involved in your theatre work be SPECIFIC!*

CHAPTER TEN

# REAL CHANGE—A STORY

## Wednesday, 20 June 1984: Daytime Session in Nature

*The more charged a text is emotionally, the less you need to do with it and the more truthful it must be.*

### Vectors in Nature

This morning, we followed Cynkutis out of the theatre and to an open area facing a field of scruffy bushes.

'Do you like to walk through the bushes?' Cynkutis asked us.

'Yes!' we said eagerly, filled with youthful enthusiasm.

'Really?' he replied quizzically, raising an eyebrow. 'Let us see what it will be like.' He gestured to the field in front of us. 'These bushes and their branches are vectors. With your body, oppose these vectors so that when you walk across the field you will not be scratched.'

We looked at the bushes more soberly now. They were close together and I could feel my body tense as I prepared to enter the thicket. No one seemed to want to be the first until Jackie forged in, moving her body swiftly, twisting from side to side, arms raised to keep them clear of the branches. The rest of us waded out into the bushes, taking different paths. I was glad I wasn't wearing shorts.

We made it through to the other side but Cynkutis encouraged us not to rest and we forged our way back again. We manoeuvred through the tangle several times, paying for any lack of attention with scratches.

‘Now repeat this exercise without the bushes, reminding your body how it was,’ he directed.

I tried to recreate the alert state needed to avoid contact with the branches, but without the original stimulus it was a messy effort. I wished I had been more aware when I first executed the task.

Cynkutis didn’t comment on our work but motioned us to follow him over to a field of tall grass.

‘Do you remember how it feels to walk through high grass?’ he asked.

This time we paused before hesitantly answering yes.

‘All right then,’ Cynkutis said, ‘Without entering the field, show me what vectors are created when walking through tall grass. What happens to your body?’

We proceeded to do an awkward mime of our bodies fighting forward against thick grass.

‘Thank you. Now walk through this field of grass.’ He motioned to the field of grass before us.

This type of grass had serrations that caused it to cling and stick. It pulled us back even as we proceeded. Now our arms weren’t hanging at our sides as they had been in our demonstrations, but lifted up and away from the rasping touch of the grass. Our upper torso instinctively created another vector as it tried to lift us out of the way. After we finished, we had to admit there was an incredible difference between what we had imagined and the reality. Cynkutis continued with the task: ‘With both the bushes and the high grass you were using vectors to protect yourself; pulling away at the same time that you are pushing forward. Without entering the grass, try to remember with your body what vectors were created. We may use this body-feeling later in the work.’

We tried to remember the physicality, leaning our torsos forward and raising our arms to assist our balance against this remembered sea of grass.

Through these exercises, we experienced how the body naturally uses vectors. Cynkutis had suggested that we remember the body-feeling in order to use it later, but for me, remembering an exact feeling or position in the body was a completely new skill. Hopefully this weak 'muscle' of body memory would continue to develop through training. It seemed an important tool for keeping the body alive and in the state of 'readiness' he had encouraged in us a few days before.

## Real Change—A Story

Cynkutis led us over to sit in the shade of a mossy glade. Once we had settled in, he began:

> There is a story that I know of two men and both of them have the same name, Mr Smith! They also have the same dream: to go to Rio de Janeiro. Mr Smith One gets a direct flight with the whole package from the brochure included: hotel, tour, meals, and organized trips. He goes to Rio and then he comes home. He has been somewhere else, but he is still the same Mr Smith. Yes, his location changed for a time, but he only moved his same buttocks from one place to another.
>
> The way of Mr Smith Two is not so easy. He learns that in Rio de Janeiro they speak another language. Imagine that! They speak Portuguese! So he goes to Portugal to study so that he can speak the language. He looks at maps of Brazil and, while looking at them, sees an interesting mountain he can climb. But he has to learn how to climb mountains. He climbs mountains in Japan and Africa and, on his way, experiences many things. It may take him a long, long time to get to Rio de Janeiro or he may never arrive, but *on the way*, he has become a different person. He has changed because of this journey, because his dream is very real to him. It is not enough to move your buttocks

> from place to place. But if you change because of your dream, many new things can happen.

I loved the playfulness of this teaching story. But it also brought stillness to the group as each of us reflected on what we would be willing to do to follow our dreams.

## Voice of Truth

'Let us work with what is around us,' Cynkutis said gesturing to the wooded glade we were in. 'Move throughout this place, and as you encounter different elements—tree, leaf, sunlight—simply name and say what you see with no interpretation, no emotion. You may say such a sentence as: "The leaf is in sunlight" or "The leaf is in shadow." '

His voice was so gently present as he introduced the exercise. He seemed to be tuning us to the deep stillness of nature around us. I loved feeling the subtle vibrations of my voice as the work proceeded. It was a delightful way to commune with the natural world.

After we had worked for a while in this way, Cynkutis called us together and we sat near him in the shade. He advised, 'In theatre if you have such a task before you as to love someone on the stage, your task is not to be in your imagination. You must still feed from your senses, drink from your senses, from the environment, from the other person.'

'What if you don't like your partner?' Judith asked.

Cynkutis paused and then said:

> If you dislike your partner, there still must be something about him or her that you like, and you must search for that and drink from that. If you need to say 'I love you' to your partner, use the previous text as a runway for that moment. The more charged a text is emotionally, the less you need to do with it and the more truthful it must be. 'I love you' becomes a sign, a symbol.

Cynkutis began speaking softly in Polish. His voice was filled with intention and unmistakable presence. It brought me to an awareness of myself, listening to the sound of his voice, here, in this moment of time. I could feel the hushed breathing of all of us gathered in the glade, sitting in a circle in the dappled light. Everyone was motionless, transfixed as his text unrolled and grew in strength. There was something quite particular in the quality of his voice, as though, through sound, he was actively searching for something. As he continued speaking, I felt a physical sensation in the middle area of my diaphragm, a touching or a movement that grew. The sensation darkened and lowered into the sinking, swooning feeling that comes with being in love. Startled, I realized that Cynkutis was working with us and on us, demonstrating that the voice could touch in such a way that it could physically create the sensation of love. It astonished me that he could do this with his voice alone, but it was happening.[1]

When he finished speaking everyone was silent. I wondered if the others had felt what I had so clearly experienced. There was no discussion though, and Cynkutis moved us on to another exercise with Voice of Truth:

> Place your back against a partner or partners. Make contact with muscles and soft parts of the body but not the bones—that can bring a drawing back that can stop the encounter. Continue with the Voice of Truth using what you encounter with your body as the source. You can say things like, 'Your shoulders are warm'—simple words. Remember this is different from trying to *do* something to your partner with your voice. Here we are simply stating the truth.

---

1 This research into deeper ways to move audience members is reflected in an interview Robert Findlay conducted with Cynkutis in May of 1982. In the interview, Findlay said: 'When I come to see your work, I'm bringing myself to your work. What your work becomes is what I am in the presence of your work.' Cynkutis replied: 'Yes. And I can try to change your presence or I can make your presence more rich. Or I can somehow stimulate you to follow my imaginations or associations' (Findlay 1987: 149).

We found partners and leaned against each other. With only the give and take of our partner's bodies, the other person seemed much more mysterious. As I worked, I felt very open to the moment, perhaps because I was still touched by what had just happened. Like when he had created a spider's web in the space, Cynkutis had again used the voice as a real force. It seemed impossible but the experience was unmistakable.

Cynkutis concluded the day's work, encouraging us to meet at the theatre for our evening session rested and ready.

CHAPTER ELEVEN

# ASSOCIATIONS

## Wednesday, 20 June 1984: Evening Session in the Theatre

> *If associations are precise, clearly and fully imagined, they open a channel of communication among the actors.*

### Body Memory[1]

When we arrived at the theatre, Cynkutis was waiting for us, energized and present, waking us up to the possibilities of the moment by his own attentive state: 'To begin our training tonight, remember the body-feeling and vectors created by walking through bushes and tall grass, and create again this work.'

We recreated our work of the morning as best we could. Apart from being physical, it was a strong exercise for the imagination and memory, requiring all of our concentration. My ability to remember how my body had responded was weak and I found myself in a disoriented, foggy state. When Jackie, moving boldly and strongly, crossed into my field of vision, it seemed like the right approach, and I tried being more active—but my work was still clumsy and unclear.

Cynkutis continued to focus our work: 'Use small elements of the plastiques to keep your body alive, remember also the experience of your senses from earlier today, the feel of the grass, the breeze, the warmth of the sun.'

---

1 For an extensive discussion of the role of body-memory in the Grotowski work, see Dominika Laster (2016: 21–56).

Reminding myself of specific sensory experiences immediately helped to stimulate my memory of the day. But adding the plastiques to this remembered activity was even more valuable. They helped me to focus on 'smaller elements', for instance the activity of a knee or an elbow, giving me something immediate and specific to focus on.

'Thank you.' Cynkutis' sonorous voice released us from the task. 'Now find the place on the stage that feels right for your tree.'

## Linking Image and Voice

As we found our places in the stage environment, Cynkutis continued to coach and guide us: 'Remind yourself of your tree, the picture of this tree and the vectors. From these vectors comes the voice of your tree. Speak as your tree.'

We did as he suggested, first finding the spot that felt right and then beginning the vector work that led into vocalization. After we had improvised in this way for a while, Cynkutis said, 'Now sit and imagine that your tree is in a dream that you are having. Speak to the tree. It will listen to you.'

We sat down where we were and soon there arose gentle, murmuring sounds as we each spoke to our tree. I could swear I felt the presence of mine.

'Now the tree is beside you and you are the voice of the tree talking to itself,' Cynkutis said softly.

Subtle impulses rippled through me as I murmured the words that came. I was in a deep, almost hypnotic, state. After quite a while in this shadowy world, Cynkutis introduced a completely different direction.

'Now I want you to take for yourself a picture, an image of a cow. What colour is it?'

'Brown and White.' 'Brown.' 'White and Black.' 'Spotted,' came our replies.

‘Your cow is now covered in mud,’ he said with a trace of provocation. ‘Say something about it.’

As we spoke about our muddy cow, a heaviness appeared in our voices and, in my case, a strong element of disdain.

With mock surprise in his voice, he said, ‘Now, your cow is peeing! Say something about it!’

Off we went in that direction! I’d never seen a cow pee and couldn’t help laughing as I experimented with the different visuals. The humour of it made me more adventurous, freeing my voice even more. It brightened our energy to realize that Cynkutis didn’t always insist on everything being precious and serious. He brought all aspects of himself to the work, encouraging us to do the same.

After the exercise, I noted in my workbook how clearly Cynkutis had shown us that the voice responds to each change in an image. He then linked our voice with the here and now of the space with a familiar exercise: ‘Place your voice in different parts of the room. Do not just imagine this but work to achieve this. You can say what you are trying to do, for example: “My voice is touching the light,” “My voice is sliding down the rope.”’

As he demonstrated, his voice seemed to actually achieve what he was describing.

We began using our voice and imagination as tools towards the goal. ‘My voice is tiptoeing across the floor.’ ‘My voice is jumping up and down,’ came the words.

‘Know exactly where you are placing your voice and what it is doing,’ Cynkutis instructed.

We strove to achieve the vocal presence Cynkutis had demonstrated when his voice had spun a dark web from one end of the space to the other. It was true that when our voices were totally engaged with a specific task, the results were powerful and authentic.

## Associating Elements of Nature

Cynkutis ended our explorations seemingly pleased with our focus and concentration. Then he gathered us in a semi-circle to watch each other's work: 'Now for a different exercise: an improvisation in pairs. Using associations, we will relate one to the other. Judith come, please, we will work together.' He continued to describe his approach:

> I am choosing for our work different elements from nature where there is already some relationship. I am taking for myself the association of the ocean and Judith will take sand. Take time to find the place for your element in this stage environment, Judith. But remember it is not only about finding the place for your element but finding this place in relation to your partner. Your body becomes the body of your element. Find the source of this image in your body so you can drink from it.

'Are we allowed to talk?' Judith asked.

'Words are not so important. Breath and sound come naturally and are OK,' he replied.

Judith lay down near Cynkutis' feet, motionless and still as though she were trying to merge with the floor. But Cynkutis was already in motion, reaching out with his arms and then pulling them in as though he were gathering all the energy in the room. His whole body was rocking back and forth, a powerful, rhythmical movement, the motion of the waves. His commitment to the task and to his image was absolute with every part of his being totally engaged. Cynkutis' strong rhythms snapped Judith out of her meditative state and she became caught up in his motion, sucked back and forth on the floor like the sand moved by the sea, subsumed by the rhythm and energy of the waves. No longer were we watching two distinct people. Each actor, completely committed to the task, was joined together by this shared image. I was reminded of the butterfly analogy Cynkutis had made the other evening, of the camouflage that makes for good acting: 'If they will sit on a rock, they look like a rock. If they will sit on grass, they look like grass.' In this improvisation, Cynkutis and Judith were not showing themselves at all; they were serving their partner, the image, and the work.

After their improvisation slowed in rhythm and came to a natural end, Cynkutis gave the rest of us elements of nature to explore with our partners, allowing us to use text and coaching us to be ever more specific: 'If associations are precise, clearly and fully imagined, they open a channel of communication among the actors.'

When my turn came, I was given cloud and my partner sun to work with. Unfortunately, when I tried the exercise, I didn't solidify the image in my own body before relating to my partner and felt completely lost. Manifesting my image vocally helped, but without it being fully rooted in the body it was not enough. The glorious merging I had just witnessed was not to be.

After we finished, Cynkutis said: 'There are many theatrical uses for these improvisations with nature. For instance, a good children's theatre would be one that uses improvisations that come from what we see in nature.'

I wondered if Cynkutis was still trying to answer the pointed question Elizabeth had asked just a few days before 'What does any of this have to do with acting in a play?' Had her question struck a nerve? Was he still trying to respond to it? Or perhaps this suggestion was part of his aim to make the Laboratory Theatre's legacy useful to all theatre practitioners including those whose work is for children.

## Associations and Text

Cynkutis focused us on our next task: 'We will now continue work with the animal associations you have chosen. Take time, please, to think what is the most expressive moment for your animal? The most expressive . . . ' He slowed the end of his question and let it hover; dropping us into the frame of mind needed to source our animals. After giving us time to reflect, he questioned each of us on what we had found. When he came to me, I said, 'When it gets caught,' remembering the quicksilver turning and panic of the salamander.

Indicating we should find a place on the stage, he introduced an additional element: 'Working with the moment you have decided upon, search to find the physical rhythm of the animal. This will influence the rhythm of the text.'

I found a space towards the back of the stage and, drawing from my earlier work, began embodying the salamander. The focus and concentration needed for the task felt like I was gathering my energy for a leap. As I conjured the experience of being caught, I was again seized by quick and frenetic energy—an explosive experience of being this salamander.

This time, I wasn't as thrown off by the intensity with which the image moved me. I spurted from the back of the stage to the front, avoiding capture. Then I darted to the back and then front again, frenetically trying to elude pursuers. When the moment of actually being caught came, I flipped over on my back, belly exposed, vulnerable and wriggling like the salamander I'd witnessed. I continued repeating this sequence using counting as my text.

I was a bit frightened at how overwhelming it all was; my body was thrust into immediate action, and when I spoke, my voice was high-pitched and constricted from tension and fear. The process was like riding a wave, requiring an unbelievable amount of energy, but I kept my focus on the image, 'drinking from it' as Cynkutis would say. My voice was loud and shrill, but I didn't care if I was doing the task right or what others might think. I just clung like a drunkard to my wild ride of a trapped salamander.

Cynkutis instructed us from the side, 'Now work with your text from *Long Day's Journey into Night*.'

I picked up my text with shaking, sweaty hands, occasionally referring to it as I worked, but these lines had the same shrill tone. I was glad when Cynkutis called for a break. I was exhausted and my muscles were aching.

'Thank you for your commitment to the task and to the image,' Cynkutis said to the group. 'And remember, it is not always that a lot of energy needs to be expressed in the work. An actor learns how to conserve his energy.'

Cynkutis walked to the centre of the space. 'Always, when doing these explorations, you are searching for moments that will connect with your text,' he said, beginning to demonstrate:

> **[Audio #5]** If I will see Mary as a bat. It is abstract this association because she is not a bat. But it will come to my mind. The very first thing which I will do will be . . .
>
> [*Cynkutis' breathing and body change as he takes on the physicality of a bat. His body turns rapidly, sending his voice in various directions.*]
>
> Hey! How are you today? How are you today? Are you there? Are you there? Where are you? Hey! Where are you? How are you today? I feel OK. Do you feel OK? I feel OK. Why are you looking at me? Why are you looking at me? What kind of a . . . what a horrible thing. Why are you looking?
>
> [*Without breaking his physicality, Cynkutis comments on what he is finding in the work.*]
>
> What I'm getting first is this . . . [*alluding to what is becoming alive in his body and voice at this moment*]. But from this *rhythm* and from my knowledge which I have that bat is using its voice as a radar, I am using my voice like a radar. Changing directions because it is an animal which is changing sometimes the directions. And I'm risking to use it to say the text. It doesn't mean it is a result. It is the very first, very imprecise form how I want to discipline my investigation. You know what I mean? It is like to take a pen into my hand. I am taking the very first pen and I am

using this pen to start my writing, improvising this scene and talking. And I am concentrated only on bat. When I will read this text of Mary for instance, with the association of bat . . .

[*Cynkutis embodies the bat again.*]

Well . . . here it is . . . here it is . . . I have it [the bat] already somehow in my body, right?

[*He continues, improvising for several minutes in Polish. Then he explains his process.*]

I am being my bat, and I am letting my voice to be like a bat, flying in the space from wall to wall. Hitting walls. Escaping from . . . from walls. Avoiding accidents. And it is the very first sketch which I am doing. If, by this work [*using the association of bat*], I will find that parts of this text somehow are matching with something that in me feels that 'Oh! It is right.' I will return to this text, to these sentences. I will try to use the association with bat less but I will ask myself: what it is . . . what it is . . . where it is . . . where it is? And if I find several forms which will touch me, which will talk to me, I will establish an association with bat. If I do not, I will leave it, and I will work again, searching, because sometimes an association, even if it looks terrific, doesn't work. It doesn't work because nothing in me was really animated by it.

'You mean if it looks terrific in your mind when you think of it?' asked Judith.

Yes, and you were trying but nothing happened. So watch, [Judith], it is almost the same as what you did on the stage when, for instance, you associated Mary with a clock. This abstraction you took seriously and that established a certain way that you spoke. It could have been plant or eagle! With this, let's say in a good sense, childish seriousness, you created a certain form. And I thought your acting really had a lot of foolish childhood games that happen. So, please, don't be afraid and let's again try to read your text. Don't hurry up. In fact, during your rehearsal, it could be *not even intended*. You can break the logic of the text, everything. Focus on your association and try to use names, sentences as sound to develop it. OK? **[End Audio #5]**

The demonstration was inspiring. Cynkutis' work seemed so free and yet it had incredible form, disciplined by the association he had chosen. We continued working into the night, searching for what our associations might bring to the text.

CHAPTER TWELVE

# TIME AS A PARTNER IN THE WORK

## Thursday, 21 June 1984: Daytime Session in Nature

> *The art of making time present is one of the most difficult parts of acting.*

### Exploring Associations in Nature

As soon as we arrived at the theatre, Cynkutis informed us that nature would be our laboratory again today. We happily followed him out to a large, flat ridge that looked out on tree-lined hills.

Cynkutis, sunlit and fully engaged, challenged us forward with the task:

> Today we will continue our work with associations. Name and touch with your voice what is around you. Do not be afraid to name something very far away such as 'hill' or 'field'. See what association you can find for it. What is it like? How is it for you? For instance, I can say that this tree is not just a tree; this tree can be fingers, or it is a brush. Explore your association. Develop it with your voice; use improvised text—whatever comes to you. It can even be that you will sing.

He turned from us and began to work in Polish. As his voice reached out to the distant hills, he seemed in deep communion with the elements he was trying to touch, staying with a part of the landscape for several minutes before moving on. Each new association changed the cadence and texture of his voice. In the end, he sang. His voice rose and fell among the hills, free but not formless because of the power and specificity of his focus.

Clearly exhilarated by the exchange, he turned back to us. 'Find your own place, and when you are ready, begin,' he prompted.

We each found a place along the ridge and began naming various elements, touching them with our voice, improvising text as we went along. As we worked, Cynkutis circulated among us, asking questions that helped us to refine our associations, coaching us to make our improvisations more specific.

After working with Judith for quite a while, he called us over to join him: 'Let us watch for a moment the work of Judith. Here you will see that in this work with association it can be that a certain rhythm comes.'

Judith's association for the distant, rolling hills was skin. As she followed the rise and fall of the land, caressing it with her voice, her text developed a rich organic pacing. Cynkutis then led us to the top of another hill from which we could see a thick parade of cumulus clouds.

## Conversation: Naming / The Energy of Decision

'What do these clouds remind you of?' Cynkutis asked. 'Once you find an association, use your voice to *name them*! Continue to develop the association with your voice.'[1]

---

1 'To be able to name . . . If someone is not able to name they are not able to create. And "name" doesn't mean to describe. To name means to associate things. By naming you are associating. If we will go back [to] how hammer . . . [came to have its] name, "hammer", it was the process of association between [the] object and what this object did. What kind of sound or what kind of material made that it got [the] name hammer . . . hammer. Rain . . . rain . . . what happens between these drops falling down from the cloud that it . . . [got the] name rain. It is [an] abstraction. Someone was in a very . . . creative moment to name it and it came to be alive. Now [it] is enough to say rain and you feel drops. It is a very important secret to see the world not as it is in stagnancy, but to try to move the world. You can move the world by naming.' (Cynkutis 1982)

We named what we saw in the clouds. 'Castle!' 'Boat!' 'Baby!' At one point, David's voice pierced through the rest. 'Duck!' he said, repeating the word several times with precision and strength. 'Duck! Duck!'

When our work session was over, Cynkutis led us back to the theatre to speak about what he had observed:

> **[Audio #6]** Today, I will use the example of the work by David: 'cloud'. By work done before and by explanation he knew—and literally he took—information on how to work, and he *punched* by his voice this cloud. Decision, determination in his voice, precision in his voice, evoked in him an image. And he created—really—this cloud to be like 'duck'. This energy, decision, and courage to touch this cloud by voice and to name it 'duck' is like an act. And later, after this act, he was drinking from his own courage and decision. Because his voice, already present in space and in time, did charge him to develop more and more. He was drinking from his own invention.
>
> If you will stay in front of the lake, if you will take a stone into your hand and you throw the stone into the water, it seems to be that the most spectacular moment is when the stone is sinking into the water. No. Maybe it is spectacular, but it is not the most interesting. The most interesting thing starts later, much later, when these wheels which are close to the stone are growing bigger and bigger and, after a few minutes, to your feet is coming the reflection of the stone which a few minutes ago sank into the water. In these waves there is a certain time. In these circles, there is a certain time passing.
>
> In acting, through comparison, it is the same. We have, with determination and courage, to select a tool and to select a task to attack our image, even if we don't believe too much. But we have to attack. Because if we do attack with our courage, if we try by our voice or our movement to reach something which seems to be impossible to reach, not the moment in which we

are *trying* is so important but this energy which *from this decision* comes to our body and comes to our voice later works for us. The actor who is in a hurry never is able to drink from this phenomenon. The actor who respects *time* is drinking from it.

That's why it is so essential to find a way how to *not* hurry, how to *not* be so fast, how to *not* speed up—in acting and in talking. Certainly it is a danger to be too slow, but it is less dangerous than to be too fast, and it is much more easy to correct.

When you were working with this text today [associating an image with the hills], after each of you did what you did, when I was somehow talking to you, I was not only providing you with more precise information, I was organizing your time. Trying to focus you on certain, let's say, *small* elements asking you to be more precise using *small* elements. I encouraged you: 'Do not run,' 'Do not escape,' to take time—and you took time. And each of you did improve the very first proposal. Time was much more important than my information. However, my information was meant to organize for you this time, to not leave you alone with the time.[2] It is something that, if it is conscious, we can control by ourselves and we don't need a director or instructor. If we are conscious, if we do really estimate highly the value of the time, it is already an important element supporting acting. **[End Audio #6]**

## Conversation: Time as a Partner in the Work

After a break in which we wrote in our journals and reflected on the work of today, Cynkutis again gathered us together for a conversation on what he viewed as the most important elements of acting:

---

2 Here, Cynkutis clarifies that our relationship to *time* was an important end result. Focusing our explorations on smaller details was his way of achieving this.

**[Audio #7]** Who knows something about acting and actors whose playing is empty? It is like a car which is running on an empty tank—it is almost sure that it will stop in one moment.

Actors who are running on a full tank means an actor who knows about work of the body, work of the voice, how associations—how images—have to provide the body and voice with certain information to get presence on the stage. Presence is a value. Those actors, they value very much *time*. They never are in a hurry.

Actors who are running on an empty tank, they don't know a lot; their experience is still very small. For them to be on the stage it is a very frightening moment because they don't want to show how little they know. [ . . . ] They are on the stage, but they are escaping from the stage. It is a typical disease for young actors if they are not disciplined by a task, if the director does not have pedagogical experience and is not able to provide them with tools and knowledge how to act. If they are on their own, without experience, usually they are fast—running.

In both examples, something is characteristic: time. For experienced actors, time is a partner. It works *for* them. They accept time. They like time. They need more of the time for themselves. For inexperienced actors time is an enemy; they want to escape from time. [ . . . ]

Everyone who is using the technique which I name: 'pumping emotions', which even physically, by getting you tired, is creating a kind of substitute for the feeling in the actor's body, is *killing* the time, not *using* the time.

Knowledge about vectors, knowledge how to drink from your own experiences, associating them with phenomena which exist in nature, for instance, knowledge how to associate the text by an author with our life, helps us to *use* time. It *needs* time. And the actor, instead of jumping onto the stage and playing, the actor is entering the stage and working. This is, for me, the most significant difference between a good approach to acting and bad. I easily can distinguish when an actor is working. A working actor needs time, because there is no good work which can be done without it.

I told you a few days ago that, in my opinion, the best attitude of an actor is to be a servant. So, with this attitude actor-servant, I want to serve for my audience *time*—the feeling of time. I am very aware of time. Why? Because I know that everything that is really valuable needs a kind of preparation—for every human being to *tune* someone else to receive values. We do miss a lot of values in our life if we don't tune ourselves to receive them. If we are, day by day, just running from one mall to another hunting for discounts, we definitely are not tuned to receive other values. And, even if close to us will be someone who can give/share with us a tremendous amount of valuable things, we don't see him/her because our focus is on discount prices, on the goods.

If we are watching our watch, swallowing tea, or coffee inside of the car, driving our car on the highway to reach the garage close to our office. We are not tuned to see the beautiful sunset or sunrise which is on the road because we are not ready. We keep ourselves away from such a value. And even if we see that this sky is incredible and we feel it is wonderful we somehow are angry that we cannot stop and admire it. We are against this wonderful sunset! We are opposite to this wonderful sunrise because we cannot stop our car in the middle of the highway and still it is! So, why is it when I cannot stop? You know what I mean? We feel such guilt—blame. We blame ourselves.

Cynkutis let the thoughts he wished to impart linger in the space before continuing:

In acting, in art, it is not only the moment in which we are on the stage but the moment when we are preparing ourselves for our part [that is important]. And if the part is already rehearsed and prepared, it is how we wake up early in the morning and how we plan the whole day facing ourselves towards evening when there will be the performance. And this focus on the evening is giving the sense for the whole day. [ . . . ] So we tune ourselves. When we tune ourselves, we do something with our life time too. So our cup of coffee, our bread, our cooking, or our resting, is not only resting, is not only a cup of coffee—everything has a certain *aim*. Everything is on the road towards evening when there will be the performance, the most important element of the day.

When we are preparing ourselves like that, even our daily time has a different time, colour, rhythm, and value than the same time of the clerk living next door. So, when we are coming to the theatre, making up, dressing or just silently concentrating ourselves on the task which is in front of us, we are dealing with the time. We need this time.

Exactly the same—however with quite different dimensions of the time—happens when we already are appearing on the stage. *We have to be present in time*. Theatre is the only art in which the presence of here and now—presence of *here* and presence of *now*—is really meeting and really is essential for art which has to happen on the stage. [ . . . ]

If I said that time on stage, is for me similar to the time which in life we feel only if we are in another state than a common state—like love or sorrow—it's exactly what I want to say. That acting is a kind of activity done by an actor in a state different from daily states. This means that when we are on the stage, we really have to find ourselves in another state. This state is not only, or necessarily, emotional. It can be an intellectual state also, but such an intellectual state has to lead us also into emotions in which our thoughts and feelings are able to meet on the stage. Each meeting is the result of activity. We can approach another state only through activity. We have actively to search how to leave a commonplace state and to achieve another.

It needs a positive, creative attitude towards acting but also knowledge: knowledge of concentration, knowledge about how to wake up the imagination, how to drink from the imagination, how to use associations and how to make transmission from everything that is somehow based on our individual personal experiences into an artistic act. [We have to know] how to discipline our emotions and feelings, by selecting the right props and using them for material which, in one case, will be a play like an Anouilh play, in another case it will be a Beckett play. And sometimes it will not be a play at all. It can be an absolutely new form invented totally by the actors and director together and that is also theatre.

I am often using a comparison [of time on the stage] with an act of love. In a real act of love, we are like discoverers because our senses are so open; we are opening our senses. Not only sense in a sensual sense, but [ . . . ] we feel the *sense* of what it means to touch. Touch is getting again a function for us. And it usually is not in a hurry; we rather want to slow down everything. It happens from the process—it is on the way. Because something from the partner that we are receiving is informing us that we have to find a stronger or softer way and instinctively you are searching for it. The dimension of the time is different. Impossible to achieve without time.

Time on stage has different dimensions, intensity, and meaning than the time which we are counting boiling our eggs or watching the number of hours at work. [ . . . ] A wounded person lying on the sidewalk feels each second a hundred times longer than really it is. Because time for someone who is very involved in something, deeply, emotionally involved, spiritually involved, not only intellectually involved, time really counts differently. [ . . . ]

Time in our daily life, common time, is usually like seconds on the watch or hours on the alarm clock. This time is rather like an organizer of our days and nights. The person who is in a certain state, emotionally and spiritually involved, feels time not as an organizer, but feels time as a certain presence. Time is present. On stage, time has to be present. Actors are making time present. The art of making time present is one of the most difficult parts in acting. **[End Audio #7]**

Before we parted, he said, 'To prepare for our work tonight, find the emotion within your text. Then choose a picture, a memory from your past that you can associate with it. See you this evening.'

CHAPTER THIRTEEN

# MEMORIES

Thursday, 21 June 1984: Evening Session in the Theatre

*Now and here is the meeting for everything that* was *to meet what* is.

## Sourcing Memories

After individual warm-ups, Cynkutis described our task: 'You have chosen a memory, a picture from the past, to associate with the text and the emotion in the scene. Speak your text and touch with your voice that picture.'

In my monologue, Mary Tyrone speaks despairingly of her crippled hands. She can barely look at them and even tries to hide them from herself. For my emotion, I chose fear and associated it with a childhood nightmare I had of a wolf lunging from under the bedcovers at a piece of bread I held in my hands. Accessing the memory still evoked terror, and as I said my text, my voice became high and pinched and my body rigid. Although I was feeling a great deal emotionally, my expression was not varied or fluid at all.

Cynkutis came over and focused the group's attention on my work. His first approach was to ask me to be more specific. 'Can you tell me what it was exactly that frightened you?'

I tried to analyse the memory but, ultimately, I wasn't sure.

'Try your text again and remember, you are not experiencing the memory right now, you are simply recalling it,' he clarified.

This direction had little impact on how I was executing the task. Whenever I tried to access the memory, I still did it in the same way and had the same stiff, frozen body and high voice.

'Only touch the picture of this memory in the past with your voice.' Cynkutis' voice was gentle but firm, bringing with it a feeling of safety.

'Touch the picture?' I asked hesitantly.

'Yes, simply touch the picture with your voice,' he encouraged softly.

The image from my nightmare was so strong that when I conjured it and tried to touch it with my voice, I still had the same strident vocal and physical reaction.

'Let us try a different way,' he suggested. 'This time do not touch the *picture* of the memory but this *moment* from the past.'

I returned to my work but did not know how to touch the moment without engaging the visuals from the dream and stiffening in response. On reflection now, I think he was asking me to evoke *myself* in that moment of the past and not the *image*. But no matter how clear Cynkutis' instructions may have been, I still couldn't change what I was doing.

He tried another way: 'Remember this event as if it were a hundred years ago.' When I followed this directive, I lost my investment in the memory and felt completely empty.

Cynkutis patiently tried to explain what he was looking for in this work with memories:

> If you think that Mary is frightened like a timid creature, you can use 'fear' and 'timidity' and search for an expression of fear. But if it doesn't *associate*, it is only 'fear' and you have your private, individual picture which stimulates in you the memory of how to have fear, but it is only your own picture. Do you understand what I mean? Be sure. If you don't understand, don't be afraid to ask.

The problem seemed to be that this 'picture', this memory of mine, was only creating a stimulus for my own private emotion and was not associating with the text or with the character of Mary. Perhaps a different memory would be more productive. Or perhaps it was not the choice of the memory but how I was accessing it.

'So fear stimulates our voice?' I asked.

'Your fear but not in a *direct* way; we are working with the *picture* which for you represents fear,' Cynkutis paused. 'You are touching this picture by your voice.' He repeated the sentence slowly and rhythmically as though it were an incantation of what he wished me to do.

Judith interrupted the moment, her eyes bright and questioning: 'But isn't acting all about using personal emotions for the part? Why can't we use our personal emotions directly?'

Cynkutis shifted his focus back to the group: 'Why is this important? Let us take time to try to understand.' He carefully communicated his thoughts:

> In art, everything that is of real artistic value is the result of transformation. We transform something that is energetic, let's say, from one reality into another; that is if we are taking life in the sense of energy. Whatever happens in our life happens once and becomes the past. When you recall this moment, it is . . . What? It is already something else. It is a source informing our work: an energy, a presence. It is not for us to have a personal experience but as material for art, for the very marrow of the work.
>
> In acting we are calling back something that *was* to be again present. We are feeling all the time this time. And we are doing something that is remarkable because we are calling from the past into the present time our emotions and using them once again. They are never the same because we transform them by mastery, art, into something else; but they are somehow presently engaged. That's why if someone is devoted to acting, they are usually, at the same time, an unusual person who has a very great sense of time, relationships, senses, spirit . . . a lot of things.

It doesn't differ from the work of a great painter or sculptor. They also are calling back from the past their experiences and their experiences from the past are leading their hands to the brush: how to cut, how to paint; not only what is now and here. Now and here is the meeting for everything that *was* to meet what *is*.

So our task is to bring back something in the past to use in the here and now.[1] And we will focus on our senses to source this memory. For example, I can remind myself of a picture and it helps to concentrate my attention.

Cynkutis begins to access a picture from his memory, showing his process in action:

[Audio #8] When I try to concentrate my attention . . . Still I don't know how to use it . . . .

[*He continues the demonstration.*]

I am talking . . . I am talking . . . I am using my voice . . . trying to touch . . . I am trying to touch the picture by my voice [ . . . ].

Or, can you imagine? It is like an abstraction, but you can touch smell by your voice. You can. It seems abstract but, no! Do you remember how cows smell? [ . . . ]

[*He focuses on using his voice to touch this smell repeating the word at the same time.*]

Smells . . . Smells . . . Smells . . . You can touch by your voice this smell, and the way that you are touching creates expression in the voice. Do you understand what I mean?[2]

---

1 For a detailed description of Thomas Richards' work with Grotowski on personal memories, see *At Work with Grotowski on Physical Actions* (1995: 57–67).

2 In an interview with Robert Findlay, Cynkutis spoke at length about sense memories and associations in acting:

> The use of associations to bring power and meaning to a text or a song was very developed in the Laboratory Theatre. The association is private

'I'm trying, but I'm not sure that smell works for me,' I say.

So, very good! Because each of us is differently oriented. For someone smell is important, for someone touch is important, for someone sounds are important, for someone taste . . . taste. Watch—if, for instance, sound is important I can imagine how an old house sounds . . . old wooden house with wind blowing through it. Do you remember those sounds? Windows . . . doors . . . everything starts to squeak. [*Cynkutis works with this association*] It makes sounds . . . squeaks . . . wind . . . doors . . .

[*Very briefly he explains what happened in his work.*]

I am touching by my speech these sounds, the imagination of the sound, and it creates a rhythm.

Taste! Taste! For instance, my favourite fruit is mango.

[*He uses his voice to conjure the taste of a mango while improvising text.*]

---

to the actor and feeds their work. Even if the association does not seem to logically relate to the overarching meaning in a piece, as long as it communicates what is wanted to the audience the actor will keep it to drink from in their work . . . . A simple example: I am in the process of creation and I am, for instance, very involved with my song I am going to sing. But my real motivation has nothing to do with the time I am in or the time I am thinking. The motivation can come simply from what is the feeling of the smell of cut grass. I am singing the song. You are listening to my song. For you my song expresses [the feeling of] war. For me the motivation is to feel the smell of cut grass. The smell of cut grass makes the song I am singing more rich. I'm not fighting to express anything about war. And later you say to me, for instance, 'It was a beautiful song. I felt the stupidness and tragedy of war in your song.' I say, 'Man, I didn't know about what I was doing. I was totally involved in smelling cut grass.' So I'm not able to say anything about war but I know how the feeling of the smell of cut grass is important to repeat [when I sing my song] if I want to make a form . . . . It has everything to do with associations. (Findlay 1987: 148–49).

Oh, I love mango: yellow, juicy, sweet . . . yellow. I love it. I really love it . . . I am trying to use my voice to touch the taste.

[*He pauses, making sure we are with him.*]

That's why, in this moment, if you are feeling that you are missing something or you are not touching something, concentrate. Take silence. Make silence. Imagine the picture—and try to touch by your voice, in this picture, something that especially speaks to your senses. Sometimes it will be a sound, sometimes it will be taste or touch.

And don't be afraid to make mistakes. Mistakes are honest . . . honest. **[End Audio #8]** If you are not afraid to make something wrong, I am able more and more precisely to develop what we are doing. Because, in each session, I am trying to find tools, something that you can train with and that can support certain work. Do not be afraid to make mistakes. It doesn't mean pushing for mistakes, certainly. Only don't be afraid.

So, everyone, touch by your voice whatever you want to use in this memory and say what comes to your mind. Don't try to make it completely ready.

I wondered what sense I should concentrate on. It was clear that just conjuring the terrifying dream image was not allowing me room to explore. Could I work with one of my sense memories from within the dream? I decided to try that approach and chose touch as the sense I would work with. In the dream, as the wolf leapt towards the bread, I had grabbed the bedcovers and pulled them up around me to protect myself. When I tried to again hold the soft bread in my hand, with it came the unmistakable smell of homemade bread. Then I remembered the feel of the bedcovers—an old-fashioned spread with soft raised areas. When I tried to pull it, I felt its softness but also an unyielding tension because my mother always tucked it in so tightly at the bottom. The tension of the covers introduced a strong opposing vector, resisting my attempt to protect myself from what was coming from below. My hands and indeed my whole body were now immediately involved. The crippled hands that Mary feared were in action, trying to save me and at the same time exposed in their helplessness. Now when I used the text to touch and explore the sensations, new meanings emerged. The memory resonated with the text, and I was at last able to explore.

We continued working with our memories, using our remembered sensory experiences and our voices to touch, looking for something that would associate with and illuminate our texts.

## Conversation: Historical / Autobiographical (I)

As we were writing in our journals after this evening's work, Judith asked Cynkutis to explain more about the Laboratory Theatre's work with personal emotions. Her questions were thoughtful and provocative: 'In the Laboratory Theatre weren't the actors supposed to be so alive on stage that it wasn't even like they were playing a part?'

Cynkutis paused, then said: 'Yes, Grotowski had this idea when he said to us, "Now stop acting. Please, no acting. Only what is real." But this also caused a lot of problems.' As he recalled this time, Cynkutis' voice had an unusual quality, full of emotion, both intimate and precise:

> To be alive on stage *without acting* means that whatever is going on is coming from your blood, from your *real* feelings, from your *real* emotions and from your *real* possibility. How you feel time and the moment and partners and people here and now. And if you are taking the text or whatever, it is only a pretext to make self-exploration, self-investigation.[3]

---

3 In *Towards a Poor Theatre*, Grotowski speaks in depth about his ideal of the 'holy actor' who 'reveals himself and sacrifices the innermost part of himself [ . . . ]' (1968: 34–39). He refers to this sacrifice as the 'Total Act'. The following fragment is especially pertinent to what Cynkutis is describing:

> But this self-exploration can also be self-aggression if you are trying to create a structure that only allows you to be like an open nervous system. You cannot tune your nervous system in such a way that whatever you are doing is not a game at all and is just *real*. It is a nice idea, but it is not realistic.

'But,' Elizabeth interjected testily, 'isn't that the same thing you asked from us? You said that when we come in here, we have to leave our problems outside the door. And when you're doing a task, you have to expose everything that you're feeling.'

'Yes, but it is a different attitude: how you are coming to this work here,' Cynkutis replied and continued:

> [Audio #9] You can always, against every feeling, leave your private feelings behind the door and show work. But you cannot expose yourself. Do you understand? It is a great difference.
>
> If I have a certain [acting] structure and if I have this security that, even if I am weak, even if there is something wrong with me, even if I don't like to work but I feel obliged to do it, if I keep

---

> [ . . . ] the decisive factor in this process is the actor's technique of self-penetration. He must learn to use the role as if it were a surgeon's scalpel, to dissect himself. It is not a question of portraying himself under certain given circumstances, or of 'living' a part; nor does it entail the distant sort of acting common to epic theatre and based on cold calculation. The important thing is to use the role as a trampoline, an instrument with which to study what is hidden behind our everyday mask—the innermost core of our personality—in order to sacrifice it, expose it. (Grotowski 1968: 37)

And further:

> Here an actor should not act but rather penetrate the regions of his own experience with his body and voice . . . [ . . . ] this is neither a story nor the creation of an illusion; it is the present moment. The actor exposes himself and . . . he discovers himself. Yet he has to know how to do this anew each time. (Grotowski, in Osiński 1986: 86)

my structure and I am very honestly trying to make this structure as alive as possible. Then I feel OK.

But if the task on me is to come and to use the structure to attack myself always and to be extremely, even with surprises, open . . . it is another pull of an extreme which is wrong. Because I am not every time able to do it. If I feel pushed to do it, I have to find a way how to play it. And if I will play myself, it is the worst acting. Because in this case I am not playing a character, I am not playing a part, I am not playing anything which is valuable. I am interpreting myself. My goodness! It is subjective up to the nonsense level.

Judith leaned forward, eyes bright, initiating another topic she had questions about: 'Why did Ryszard Cieślak[4] become the name that we heard the most?'

Ah, you see it is simple, because, in 1959 when Grotowski started his company, he was focusing on one actor. This actor was Zygmunt Molik, and Zygmunt was playing the main parts. Grotowski always was working mainly with one actor.

'Why?' David asked. Cynkutis continued:

I really don't know why. When I came, I became his beloved actor so, till '63, every main part I was playing. In that time, we made *Forefathers*, [*Kordian*,] *Akropolis*, *Idiot*, and *Dr. Faustus*. *Dr. Faustus* opened the door for the company abroad, to Paris and to every other country in Europe.

In 1963, I had a very big crisis. I was not able to work anymore with Grotowski, no more with this group. I felt crushed and I left the company. I went to another town. I didn't even want to stay in the same town. I returned to the conventional

4 Ryszard Cieślak's performance in *The Constant Prince* was an international sensation. He became Grotowski's most famous actor, travelling with him internationally to demonstrate the work and lead trainings.

theatre, working with conventional actors and playing again a lot of parts in a conventional, professional theatre.

This time, Grotowski, who always wanted to pick one actor to focus on; he selected Cieślak. But the doors to our theatre were already opened [internationally] and Cieślak, who was playing as Molik before me, played the main parts, which *later* were most visible because we started to travel. Molik also left the company when I did. Molik and I were not able to continue; it was very deep. Done—at this time.

Grotowski found that he is not able to work without us so he called us back.[5] And it was not so easy to return. But, at the same time, we had very big respect for everything that was our work done before and the perspective of the work by Grotowski. So we returned, Zygmunt and I. We came back in 1965 and we started again everything. Together we have done the last performance, *Apocalypsis cum Figuris*, and that's it.[6] We stopped acting. We stopped making performances by the whole company. Since 1970 starts paratheatrical theatre. Everyone had his own field and his own laboratory inside of the Laboratory Theatre, leading very individual work.

So if there will be another actor after Ryszard it will be the same. Because Zygmunt's work, my work, Ryszard's work, will work for the next one. We did learn from one another and no

---

5 Grotowski built his work and his approach over time. For him, this required always utilizing the same company of actors. In his essay 'From the Theatre Company to Art as Vehicle' he writes: 'To draw nearer to this special approach, it was necessary to work with the same persons, the same company. [ . . . ] There are many elements related to craft that need long term work. And this is possible only if the company exists' (in Richards 1995: 118).

6 *Apocalypsis Cum Figuris* was Grotowski's last work as a director of theatre productions. It premiered in 1969 and toured Europe and the United States between 1969 and 1980.

> one of us is able to say that what I know is only mine. It is the experience of everyone.[7]

Judith continued to try to understand how Grotowski worked with his actors: 'Did Grotowski work with you on the floor, moving, and with his voice?'

> He did. There was such a period in his life that he was active, but it was a short time.

'Did he have ideas for you? Or tasks? Directions?' she asked. Cynkutis tried to clarify what was clearly a complicated situation:

> He has a very good sense of what is possible, and he, through other people, is able to lead work. That's why he always needs someone who will work with him extremely closely, who will be like his body.
>
> So if he is using other people, it is not something that he is doing for his private purpose. It happens to him because he wants to go as far as possible and to explore as much as possible. **[End Audio #9]** Well, we will meet again tomorrow.

---

7 Because of lack of documentation, it is hard to trace the indirect transmission from Grotowski's first company of actors to his later work with Thomas Richards, Grotowski's actor-collaborator in his final phase of research: Art as Vehicle. But it is interesting to note some unusual similarities in Cynkutis' and Richards' writing about process. Speaking of his work on the role of Faust, Cynkutis mentions the importance of an interior opposition of forces of 'using the two opposite psychic impulses of "may" and "may not"' (2015a: 163). Discussing the transformation of energy in his work with traditional songs, Richards also speaks of the importance of opposing forces, in this case calling them 'yes' and 'no': '[ . . . ] the process with the song is looking to change something in you. In you there will be yes/no, yes/no, yes/no [ . . . ]' (1997: 68–69).

### Journal entry, evening of 21 June 1984

*Interesting how this one memory from my childhood had so much power. But it does seem that the focus on the senses—leading me away from a big emotional recall into remembering something sensual—showed how a memory, even a terrifying one, could influence the work without overwhelming it. After today's session, I felt clear that what we want to achieve is never just a personal experience but to somehow transform that material into art, into something greater.*

CHAPTER FOURTEEN

# THE ATMOSPHERE OF A PLAY

## Friday, 22 June 1984: Daytime Session in Nature

> *In each good play* [ . . . ] *it is not the story that is important but a certain process which is captured by the dramaturgy. A process in which certain energies are released.*

### Capturing a Play's Atmosphere through Activity

This morning, Cynkutis brought us back to the field at the base of the hill. The day was oppressively hot so he gathered us under the great, solitary tree. As we sat in the shade beside him, he introduced us to today's work:

> When you are acting you can feel, and you need to feel, the atmosphere of an act—the entire act or scene or the whole play. For example: it is impossible to play Brecht if you don't capture the particular atmosphere of his play. *The Threepenny Opera* [1928] has a certain character. This character is incredibly important, and an actor has to use his talent and abilities to create it. At the same time, the actor needs to make wise choices and not do everything that comes to mind. Even a great acting possibility cannot be used if it doesn't fit with the particular expression of the play. Usually, the person who is responsible for the character of a play is the director.[1] But it can happen that the director

---

1 In the interview for Dunkelberg's PhD dissertation, Mancuso relays a conversation she had with Cynkutis. Dunkelberg contextualized the conversation:

doesn't feel it. Now there are so many directors who, quite simply, do not know what they are doing.

Something that usually helps us to find this feeling is a kind of intellectual work like associating scenes. For instance, if you read *Long Day's Journey into Night*, the very first scene doesn't really speak about anything dangerous. But something is in the air even though nothing explicit is said about the problem—still something is in the air. This means that the very first scene needs to provide the actors, and has to provide the audience, with preparation for everything that comes later. What can you compare this scene with?

He began listing the elements in the scene:

Mary is happy. The boys are talking outside. Tyrone is talking with Mary. They are waiting at the table for the two sons to come. 'Why did you laugh?' 'Oh, I know they make jokes about me always.' There is something like the beginning of aggression, right? Try to say what kind of weather you can compare to this very first scene.

Judith responded immediately:

I know what I think of. There are several kinds of weather before a storm. Just before a storm, when it gets so still, is too dramatic

---

Kim Mancuso was just beginning a production of *Romeo and Juliet* at Bradford College, and asked Zbigniew Cynkutis for some directorial advice: 'I remember [telling] Zbyszek: "I don't even know where to begin with this play." Because it was so huge for me. He said, "Well, what's the most important scene?" And we talked about what I felt was the most important scene. Then he said, "What's the most important text in the scene?" So I told him what I thought was the most important place in the text. He said, "What's the most important image in that text?" He was telescoping this whole, huge, five-act Shakespearean drama down into this one image. And he said, "That's the heart of the production." He was teaching me about directing, from his point of view, as much as he was teaching me about acting [ . . . ].' (2008: 538)

> for that scene. But maybe the kind of weather that comes two hours before a storm, when the leaves on certain trees turn over onto their white side; nothing violent, but enough so you know it's going to rain. Or, if you live in the country, you see that three or four hours before the storm, cows do something strange; they all start to come together in a certain area. Usually they're scattered dots across the field. So moments like that, with the leaves and the cows—enough to make you wonder what's going to happen.

Cynkutis seemed pleased with her response: 'OK, it's a very good picture: a few hours before the storm. Well, let's try to use it. Leave your notebooks here.' He led us halfway up the hill:

> I do not want this proposal to be something for you to 'show' or to express. I rather want you to investigate. And don't be afraid of what it looks like. You can even have the feeling that you are doing nothing. Don't be very fast with judging or making conclusions.
>
> Like cows on the field that usually are like dots . . . Take different places in this area and find whatever you can do: some of you can collect flowers, some of you can just walk, some of you can relate to the trees you select, some of you can sing songs to the trees. It doesn't matter what you are doing, only please don't pretend that you are cows! It is only an image that you are like cows that are like dots in the whole area.
>
> At the same time, try to imagine that between you is something like the polarization of two magnetic poles, a plus and a minus, that are pulling one to another. So, not fast, but slowly, you try to get closer to someone. But when you get very close, the poles are turning against each other and they become two minuses that pull you back from each other and you move away—but never as far as it was before. When you are far, there is again this magnetic pull that is drawing you back towards

> somebody. But when you are getting close to someone, again it is like two minuses or two pluses—something pulls you away. But 'away' means always to find something. For instance, you find a spot where you want to roll or a place where you feel you want to run, so you are running away. But when you are away, again there is something that pulls you back. You want to be closer. Try to improvise for a few minutes such a situation on the field in which you are away, then closer, away, closer. OK? That's it.

As I looked for my place on the hill, I felt emotionally distant from everyone. I didn't enjoy group exercises and wished I could be exploring alone. But then I realized that I could use this feeling of being against the group as my polarization. I wandered away from them down the slope and over to a field of wild brush.

Looking up, I could see the others scattered across the hill. Where would I find the impulse to be attracted to them? Then a movement caught my eye. Further up the hill, Judith and David were moving steadily towards each other. It made me feel curious about why they were meeting. Could that curiosity be a magnetic pole? I walked a bit towards them and then, instinctively, matched my pace to theirs. They sensed me coming and moved to include me as well. When we were close enough to distinguish each other's features, our motion towards each other faltered and we drifted away. A strange dance on the hill developed as various group members came together and then separated in configurations of twos or threes. It seemed forever until our entire group of five was close enough to have some kind of unity. At that point, Cynkutis changed the focus of the improvisation: 'Now it is not the poles of the magnet that are pulling you one to the other. You are pulled because you are lonely, and you need to be close.'

I had become so tuned to the authoritative way Cynkutis gave instructions that the moment he gave a direction, I experienced it. I immediately felt an ache, a deep physical and emotional need, and moved closer to the others. But as we came together, Cynkutis again gave us a new focus: 'Now you are cows trying to get shade from each other's bodies.'

This suggestion fed into our real need to escape from the oppressive heat. It also gave us a clear physical focus and a competitive edge that had not been there before. Now, we were strongly out for our own needs and comfort.

'Make a sound as though you are a thousand flies on the roof of a house,' he commanded.

A low buzzing started to develop in the group.

'Some of you are flies landing upon each other and some of you are cows looking for shade or being bit,' he asserted.

We were in motion now—milling, stirring, turning, buzzing.

'Speak as a group of humans, but with this fly voice that has come from the sound you created.'

We were galvanized by the progression. Cynkutis had methodically built our improvisation into a frenzy in which we were released into the images—beyond strategy and thought. Our sound and movement continued to rise in pitch and intensity until it reached a zenith. It plateaued there for several minutes until at last it subsided. The improvisation was at an end.

As we rested, I reflected on what we had just been through. Certainly today's work was a dynamic exploration of possible relationships, but was any of this related to *Long Day's Journey into Night*? As the director, Cynkutis would have to determine what would be useful. He then focused our attention on another play:

> In Eugene O'Neill's play *Desire Under the Elms* [1924], there is another kind of atmosphere, a sexual atmosphere and energy. It is under the surface, but it is there and it is vital. Using the curves of the landscape, let us see how we can explore this. To begin,

> follow the shape of the hills with a motion that starts in the base of your spine; your body and your arms will follow.

We all did as he suggested. For me, having an undulating impulse from the base of the spine out through the arms to follow the curving landscape brought a rhythmic, sensual feeling.

'Now let your hands and your arms be still and let your body alone follow this line,' Cynkutis directed.

This felt inhibiting to me. Like a truncated torso, I now had no easy way to send this energy out from my body, but the next progression helped me build the energy to release.

'From this motion in your body, find a walk and then a run. Run along the line of the hills and let your feet feel the ground. Let your body take in the energy of these hills.' As he finished speaking, Cynkutis reached out to the hills, releasing us into the landscape.

After our lengthy, group improvisations, it was so freeing to run along the ridge, following its dips and swells, tuned to our beautiful surroundings and the voluptuous energy of desire. It was a glorious way to end the day.

CHAPTER FIFTEEN

# LIFE FORCE

## Friday, 22 June 1984: Evening Session in the Loft

> *The further you go in training, the more you increase your ability to go beyond.*

This evening, Cynkutis asked Jola to lead the warm-up section of our workshop. She demonstrated how the plastiques come alive when fed by image and intention.

### Plastiques: Image and Intention

Without speaking, Jola wove around us, bringing us into the present moment with her own presence, indicating that we were to join her on the stage. Her eyes were alive with mischief. She first demonstrated the plastiques; they flowed through her body with clearly articulated precision, animating it. Using the various rotations, she began to trade energy with us and we joined in. 'Exchange energy with a partner,' she coached. We worked in this way for some time until she indicated that we were to quiet down the movements.

When we were almost still, she gave us an image to inform the plastiques, 'Imagine that you are inside a block of ice. Feel the cold. How do you move in this ice? Feel the resistance.' Although we were barely moving, our energy was strongly engaged because of this struggle against the imagined ice.

After we explored this image for a while, she gave us an intention: 'Now, somehow you must melt your way out of this ice.' Jola demonstrated the exercise and the quality of her bodywork—focused yet free—was inspiring. Even when working with the rotation of one part of her body, every other part of her was still engaged.

Jola finished her exploration and then moved to the side to watch our work: 'Begin your rotations slowly,' she instructed. 'They are awakened by the warmth of fire coming to one part. Where does the fire begin?'

As we explored, she continued to coach us: 'The fire is rising. Moving and changing through the body. Melt this ice.' We continued our work, becoming freer with our movements as fire overtook the ice. Jola urged us on: 'The fire flows from one part to another and each part can burn. Release this fire into the space!' Soon we were as if on fire, moving with abandon, burning up the space. She counselled us to be as clear as possible in our work: 'Find something to put on fire. Be specific. Know how you are affecting it. How it feels to you when you touch it with your fire. How does it become one with you when you are both on fire?' The work was engaging and exciting. In those moments I clearly felt how image, intention, and specificity galvanized the work.

As we rested after the exercise, I wrote a note in my work journal: 'Focus on a concrete task or image. What we clearly imagine *lives*!'

Before she left, Jola and Zbyszek spoke together quietly. It was clear that there was so much that needed to be done for their upcoming journey back to Poland.

After Jola departed, Cynkutis elaborated on the importance of always linking our explorations with the body with our inner life:

> We must never approach our task like it is some kind of gymnastics even if the task is very physical. We must always be open to the life that we have inside us, using associations or exploring an image that appears in our work. Today we will use as our tool an exercise that has several functions: it develops energy within the body, and increases the range and strength of the body. How far can you go? The further you go in training, the more you increase your ability to go beyond.

## The Cat: Life Force[1]

Cynkutis demonstrated as he spoke:

> Lie face down on the floor with your arms extended straight in front of you. It is summer, hot, you are a huge cat up on a rooftop, very lazy. All of you: head, hands, chest, elbows, hips, knees and feet are very heavy. Mice dance around you. You are hungry, but you are too lazy to react.

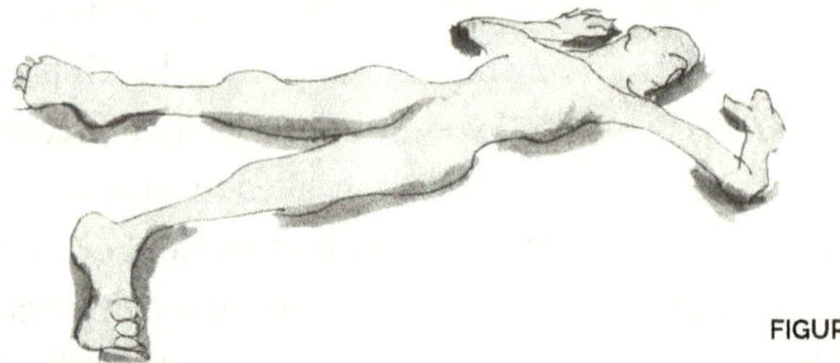

FIGURE 6

> Slowly, your hands slide down beside your face, palms flat, elbows up. A motion starts from your hips, rolls up your spine, and lifts up your head. Begin to rotate your head around watching the mice.

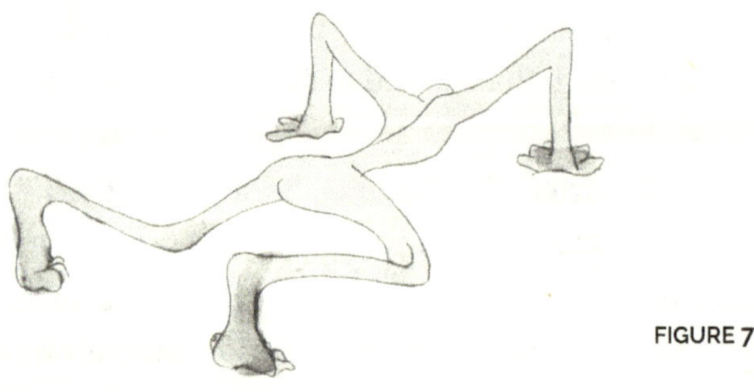

FIGURE 7

---

**1** The Cat, based in yoga, was developed by Cynkutis into a Laboratory Theatre training exercise. Illustrations, created by Bill Ireland under Cynkutis' direction, can be found in *Acting with Grotowski: Theatre as a Field for Experiencing Life* (Cynkutis 2015: 142–44). Select illustrations are reproduced here with the permission of Anna Cynkutis. My description of Cynkutis' teaching of the Cat is augmented by detailed notes made by David Russell (1983).

Now knead the floor with your hands and feet. Bring energy . . . getting ready . . .

Bang! You have dynamite under your sex [pelvis] exploding you upwards! Your pelvis is high in the air, body like a triangle with your tailbone at the top.

FIGURE 8

Swing the hips in a circle down and back up to the top again. Circle them wide in both directions ending with your tailbone again at the top.

Snap! Lift one leg off the floor, bending it and pulling it up near your body—knee close to your shoulders. A dragon is pulling your foot, but your thighs resist. Struggle till you kick off the dragon. Put that leg back down and rotate the hips around again in as wide a circle as you can.

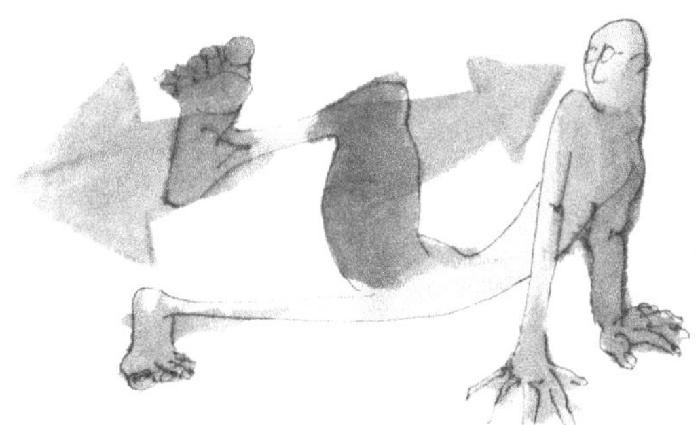

FIGURE 9

Snap! Another leg up! The dragon behind you pulls on it. Kick it away! Repeat with both legs, rotating the hips in between.

[*It seemed that every muscle—indeed Cynkutis' whole being—was engaged in the struggle with this dragon.*]

Again, circle the hips to the top of their arc and keep them suspended at their highest point. Your body forms a V shape, with the buttocks at the top. The back is straight. Imagine there is a tiny silver ball at the base of your spine and you are using your body to roll it from the bottom of the spine to the base of your neck.

FIGURE 10

Roll it back and forth several times. Feel the impulse from the base of the spine as it travels up and then down. Catch this silver ball in the small of the back and then an impulse from your buttocks flings it away.

FIGURE 11

Finish by pushing up and off your hands until you are sitting back in a crouch with all of your weight on your feet. Rest in this crouch, feet flat on floor, head down, arms loose.
(Russell 1983: 2)

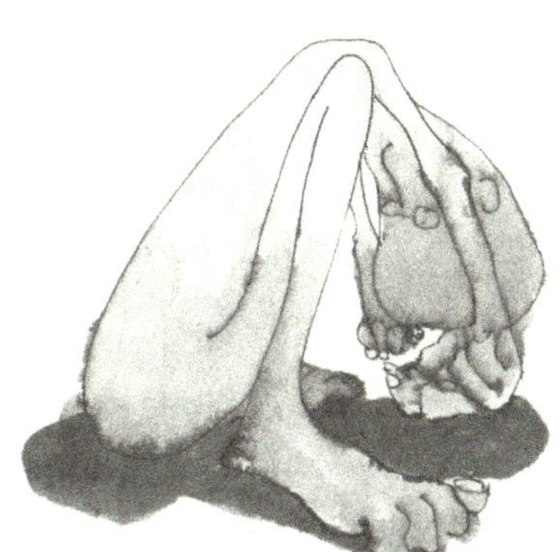

FIGURE 12

We found our places to work and began our journey through the different stages of the Cat, trying to attack it with the energy and decision we had just witnessed. It was a strenuous exercise, but whenever the associations were alive, we were able to move beyond the gymnastics Cynkutis had cautioned against and into a living moment. We worked until our palms were sweaty from the effort, swinging our hips up and around yet again, our hands almost slipping from under us. At last, Cynkutis called us to rest and we collapsed, exhausted.

'Do not forget this exercise. It is very useful in keeping the body alert. It is something I do each morning to keep my training alive, always taking as a partner those things that I see and hear around me,' he concluded.

## Conversation: Historical / Autobiographical (II)

As we were resting after the exercise, Judith asked, 'Can you tell us how you came to be part of the Laboratory Theatre?'

'Yes, I can tell you,' Cynkutis replied wryly.

As he told us his story, it was as though he were living it all again. He spoke with vulnerability, honesty, and ironic humour.

> Before I was with them, I was already working in the theatre and had also graduated with my MFA from Łódź Film School—the department for film and theatre acting. After graduating, I went to a huge, very conventional theatre. In one season, which was ten months, I was playing twenty-five parts among them three main parts.
>
> It was like a prison sentence. I was tired, smashed, crushed, and disappointed. I felt that what I learned in school is not what is really in theatre and I was close to giving up. Because what happened to me probably happens to a lot of young men. I was handsome, with blonde hair and a nice look, so they were always providing me with parts that were romantic. They were taking what nature gave to me, not asking me to improve my nature or to learn what my nature is like. So I was very disappointed and, really, I had already made the decision to give up. However, I was still on the stage and playing a lot of things.
>
> Well, I was tired, returning from my performance to my house, hating somehow work in the theatre. And maybe around midnight, someone was knocking at my door. I opened up the door and behind the door I saw a very large man with black glasses.
>
> 'I am Grotowski, Mr Cynkutis, I have here in the same town a Theatre of Thirteen Rows and I have a problem . . . May I come in?'
>
> I knew he was Grotowski because I saw him several times on the street. I heard that he is doing crazy theatre, even though I never had time to see what they were doing because they performed on the same evenings as I did.

I said, 'Come in.' He had with him such a huge script. He said, 'You know, it is really very funny, because we have four days until our opening and one of my actors playing quite a big part in my play got drunk and disappeared. Could you replace him? I saw you several times on the stage and I would like you to do it. I think you can do it.'

I said to him, 'Well then, I will have to read what it is.'

'Oh, it is a play which you know very well, because it is one of the most beautiful plays, it is *Forefathers' Eve*.' [*Dziady* (1822)]

Wow! The most important play in Polish dramaturgy! 'And what would you like me to play?'

'The Sorcerer.'

Wow! It was like the second main part. I forgot about only four days till the opening! But I had a responsibility to my company, so I said, 'Mr Grotowski, I would like to try, but I don't know if I can. You have to talk with my artistic director because I do belong to his theatre and, according to law, I cannot work in another one at the same time.'

'Oh, be sure I will do it. I know him. We are friends.'

So, he went. **[Audio #10]** I opened the text. The text was wonderful. I started to read and I made a decision. I have to do it. Even if the artistic director will not say yes, I feel I have to do it because it is like luck knocking on my door.

I was tired, but I started to learn the text. The text is poetry, but beautiful poetry. So I didn't sleep. I learned it by heart. That morning, he phoned me that my artistic director confirmed that I can do it. So I learned and in three days I memorized quite a large text. When this text was done by me automatically, I had two rehearsals and—however it was not four days but six days—after six days we opened the performance. I did this part very badly, but I saved their performance. So when the opening was done, I don't really know how I was functioning.

'Physically?' Judith asked.

Physically. They took me to the hospital because I was like a dead person. My nervous system kept me going up to the moment when it was done. When it was done, I released everything. I spent two days in the hospital, but we did it! And those guys in his company, I think that they were very impressed with what I did. They started to say to me, 'Zbyszek, why don't you stay with us?' And, at the end of the season of '60–'61, I made the decision [to stay]. However, he [Grotowski] helped me to make this decision.

He was talking to me and they were talking to me but talking, it was not enough. One day, he came with a play, *Kordian* [1889] by Słowacki, which is another play every young actor can dream about, and he said, 'I want you to play Kordian. Here is the text.' I opened the text and there was a dedication: 'For someone who is very close and dear to me with best wishes and congratulations for a long trip and work around the play—Grotowski.' So I stayed. It was exciting.

'During this time, beside performances, when did all this exploration come about?' asked Judith.

[*Cynkutis said softly*] We worked sixteen hours a day.

'Sixteen hours a day!' Elizabeth exclaimed in disbelief.

Sixteen hours a day. We slept barely six hours—maybe four or five hours. It was an incredible seven years of exploration into the mental, psychological, physical material by each of us. Grotowski didn't know anything. He learned everything from us and from our devotion. Certainly it served him how we were working and he was getting from us such gifts as everyone gave. He learned. He is talented. He is a genius. He learned tremendously fast. And very quickly he was like a person who is breathing knowledge . . . Incredible work. Incredible experiences.

Twenty-five years together. But you know, this togetherness it didn't mean friendship. There was understanding and fights too. But even if we didn't like one another, if we hate one another, we never used our private feelings in the work. We were always able to leave it behind the door. When work started, there was no hate or love. We disciplined ourselves tremendously.

'As a group did you stumble upon things accidentally, like the voice?' Judith asked.

Oh, a lot of things happened.

'How many women in the group?' Jackie asked.

There is only one, but we had in our history all together four. Only one [Rena Mirecka] stayed to the end. But you cannot imagine what kind of an experience she was. You cannot imagine what kind of presence she is able to bring.

I made one performance in which she performed. I directed the performance. I took her with me from our company to another town in Poland. I took six actors from the conventional theatre. She was playing the main part with six actors who had never worked with her. I did this because for me it was interesting to see how—through the actor, not through directing—how I can stimulate other actors to achieve, very quickly, very high skills. She was playing Yerma, in the play *Yerma* [1934], an incredible play by Garcia Lorca.[2] The rest of the cast were people who had never worked in any other style than very conventional theatre.

So, I started directing. I worked with her, on stage, preparing her part, but I made with her a commitment that, even if she

2 Cynkutis' adaptation of the play *Yerma* was titled *Jałowa* [Barren].

knows what to do, I will explain to her what she is supposed to do so they [the other actors] will listen to what I am going to ask her. And later, when she did what I asked, they were able to see how she transforms tasks into acting. When the performance was done, the whole cast said that never in their life had they had such an intensive theatrical experience as with her. I was not important; she was important. They simply fell in love with her, and they didn't want to let her go. They wanted her to stay to play every main part in the whole repertoire forever because they were drinking from her, and she was giving them a possibility to drink from.

An incredible person. A lot of things which formally we developed, about form, came straight from her. She invented a lot of forms. We never were able to guess that such a possibility existed and it was coming from her body and from her imagination. Incredible. I think that because Grotowski was not open enough to women, we never got more women. But we were very lucky getting her, because what we got from her is like thirty percent of everything that we invented. And everything that she brought was very female, based on very female imagination . . .
**[End Audio #10]**

Cynkutis closed the day's session with a promise to meet the next morning.

### Journal entry, evening of 22 June 1984

*Zbyszek is so open talking with us. What he says about Rena makes you realize how startling she must have been to work with. In a previous workshop I took with her, as we were improvising, I had an image that I was bathing a stone in water which then came to life in my hands. Rena had been sitting to the side watching us. Her presence was so strong. When she saw that moment, she entered into the improvisation, gathering the others around the awakened 'stone' that I held, moving it into an ecstatic parade around the space, a celebration of the stone which was raised on high, a heightened group experience. Rena held the key to 'events'.*

CHAPTER SIXTEEN

# ASSOCIATIONS AND SCENE WORK

## Saturday, 23 June 1984: Daytime Session in the Loft

> *To associate means to find a picture which may not* strictly *connect with the scene but, my goodness, how it connects* psychologically.

### Embodying Emotions

As soon as we placed our belongings down, Cynkutis galvanized us forward:

> Begin by walking around the space. Walk quickly, changing your direction often; it can be even at the last moment just before you crash into someone. When I call out the name of an emotion, in that moment, freeze into a statue of that emotion. Stay in that form, that statue, until I say to you again, 'Walk!'

We set off, walking rapidly, changing direction often and quickly. Cynkutis called out the names of emotions: 'Jealous! Happy! Sad!' But we were sluggish in our responses. I couldn't seem to shake off the fog I was in. I kept trying to conceive of the statue I would create before I created it. So much time elapsed between Cynkutis' naming of the emotion and my physicalization that my work had absolutely no spontaneity. 'Respond without thinking!' Cynkutis called out. 'Frightened! Crazy! Love!' His words rang out like commands. 'Walk faster! Faster!' He kept increasing our speed until we were almost running. All the while, he called out the names of different emotions until, at last, the gulf between hearing and embodying disappeared.

'Now bring chairs and sit facing a partner or partners,' Cynkutis directed. 'As I name an emotion, create the energy of this emotion between you. Source the emotion in the form of your body first, then keep it alive.'

Cynkutis called out from the side: 'Tired! Exhausted! Joyful!' One by one we attempted to create the energy of each feeling in the empty space between us. Having a partner to play against made the exercise fascinating. Could we create the raw energy of these feelings? It seemed as though it was not only possible but that it was actually happening. After a time, Cynkutis asked us to include vocalizations and the emotions became even fuller. Depending on the emotion, the seat of the voice was in different areas of the body, containing a completely different tone and energy.

I was intrigued by how Cynkutis was working with emotions, sourcing them in a configuration of the body, always stressing that we should not think, but surprise even ourselves with what emerged.

## Associations and Scene Work

Cynkutis then continued his instruction from the day before on the dramaturgy of a play:

> In each good play—in each Shakespeare, Molière, Goldoni, or Beckett play—it is not the story that is so important, but a certain process which is captured by the dramaturgy. A process in which certain energies are released: bad energy that someone is killing someone, good energy when someone is loving someone, bad energy if someone is playing games and making intrigues, good energy if someone is showing a kind of tolerance and mercy. But those are energies. And it is not so important how handsome or nasty the actor is playing a certain part, what is important is how this actor or actress is able to release this energy of *now*.

> The other morning, we spoke of the atmosphere of a play. We searched by associating the opening scene of *Long Day's Journey into Night* with a kind of weather: the calm before the storm. Let us continue to explore scenes in the play using associations, comparing them with another situation.
>
> Today, I will make another proposal: to associate scenes from *Long Day's Journey into Night* with the waiting room in a railway station. The people are waiting for a train in this empty place for, let's say already seven hours. Maybe the train will never come. In a way, their waiting is hopeless, although the situation of people waiting for a train means some kind of hope. Can you find another image, another association for people who are together in a similar way? Perhaps you will find something that will be even more powerful for you.

'It sounds like being trapped in an elevator,' Jackie suggested, 'where you're with people but it's very uncomfortable and everyone's avoiding everyone else.'

'There's not enough air,' I said, 'and even if there is, you're afraid there won't be.'

Cynkutis concluded the discussion with: 'So, let us improvise using this association. Come together please and bring objects to create this elevator.'

Using large wooden cubes, we boxed ourselves in and began to explore what this association created in us organically. The forced physical proximity felt uncomfortable and claustrophobic. I immediately wanted to escape from the others. As the scene went on, Cynkutis prompted us to release sounds. Muffled, anxious utterances and sharp intakes of breath came in response. Though the situation only lasted several minutes it felt like much longer. Cynkutis continued:

> Now, using what is in the space and without any kind of expectation, make something that can be like a waiting room in a

> railway station. If it works for you, you can bring your work with the association of being stuck in the elevator into this situation. Bring also your texts.
>
> This railway station is a place of no commitments. You can say whatever you want. You can confess the biggest sin! You can tell anything because you will never see this person again; each witness will be lost along the way. It is like a jungle in which you meet someone for the first time and then never again because of the presence of this transportation that is taking you from one spot in your life to another, through the jungle of life in which everyone can be lost.
>
> Prepare the stage for an improvisation with exactly these things: waiting for a train—railway station—no commitments. You may also bring objects into your work.

Light jackets and outer sweatshirts became coats for travellers. Tote bags and other articles became the luggage. One person picked up a broom and became the person sweeping up the station. As the improvisation unfolded, we would glance at each other and then glance away, caught in a dreamy, drifting state. No one seemed to feel the need to talk or confess.

Cynkutis began exhorting us to share our texts: 'Your text is your confession!' One after another, and sometimes two together, he called out the names of our characters and we blurted out our texts. There was a kind of desperate urgency to our work now, as though the shock of hearing our character's names compelled us to share hidden secrets. After the improvisation, Cynkutis gathered us together. As he shared his reflections with us, he also analysed how to work with scenes and associations:

> When I made my proposal—to compare scenes from *Long Day's Journey into Night* to a waiting room in a railway station—I then asked you to associate it with a stronger picture. You selected 'stuck in an elevator' and you did work with this proposal. I then asked you to create the reality of a railway station and, even

though I said that you can bring your work from your improvisation with the elevator into this new scene, you were not bringing it. Your design of the railway station, luggage and props that you brought, made this place a more powerful picture for your imagination. This association of the railway station really provided you with something and it was working for you. The elevator disappeared and you selected from these two associations the railway station because it helped each of you to say your text with a lot of variety.

At first you were not saying anything, just moments of being alone and occasionally looking at each other. Then, in one moment, I switched things. I said: 'Text Mary! Text Jamie!' and you started to improvise. In the beginning it was nothing extraordinary. You didn't know how to deal with it. There was even confusion as you thought: 'My text doesn't fit.' 'He is just calling names, jumping from one person to another!' 'What is going on?' 'Why is he doing that?'—confusion. But I didn't stop. I didn't explain anything, I let you continue. Somehow, you instinctively started to deal with the task and you associated. You didn't worry about the play. You used your text in the improvisation that was at hand and you associated two different tasks into one.

I told you the railway station is a place of no commitments. That's why people on the train tell incredible stories, because of this primeval feeling, this archetypical situation of 'wanderers on the road', two Bedouin riders or two people in the forest who are meeting and again splitting. This situation is creating in us something special: a kind of honesty, a need to talk, a wish to be with someone, to touch someone with what is inside of us or to be touched by someone. So it is a kind of extreme state psychologically. Mary is in such a state. Her train is the drugs taking her away from reality, and she has such a moment of confession.

She needs to find a witness. She needs to meet with someone and to talk. She finds Cathleen. But Mary's time is already running out. Everything in her is in motion, right?

Cynkutis turned to David who was working with the character of Jamie:

When Jamie is talking with Edmund, he is drunk. He also wants to make this confession for the first and maybe last time in his life. Like on this train, each meeting is for the first and last time. You will never meet these people again.

When you were saying the text, Elizabeth, there started a kind of game, a kind of pretending of an actress on the stage, but it was not stage acting. It was a human game filled with laughter and sounds. So from your own work and from observation, you know something more about the state of Mary, right? You found out that she is laughing. You found that she is not only talking, she is making sounds, 'Ohhh . . . Ooohhh!' She is alive. She is confessing and she needs someone to talk to.

'Yeah,' agreed Elizabeth, 'and in the play it seems like nobody is listening to anybody, but they say they are. Same here. I would say something, and people would just start in . . . '

So you actively associated. It seems to be very far from *Long Day's Journey into Night*, this picture of a railway station, but logically—oh, logically it is perfect. If a director or someone gives you such a task and you can use it, great!

So the question is: How to search for such an association? That is the question. The answer is: to read, for instance, part of the text of Mary or to read part of the text of Jamie. Find a place in the text which you like—don't focus on parts that you don't like—it is important to know what moments you like and to focus on that. Ask yourself: What is it that I like? Usually, you can easily find that you like certain affects or certain very obvious expressions and that is the very first answer that comes. Obvious. So if you feel that it is an affect or an obvious expression, don't be satisfied. Ask questions: What can I find that is deeper in this moment? What can I find deeper about Mary? I know the scene takes place in a living room . . . I [Mary] am talking to my servant . . . But what is going on? I am talking . . . my mind is wandering . . . It is just confusion, nothing else.

No! It is not just confusion because one of the most interesting ways to approach your work is not to let yourself be trapped by everything you can easily read from the text. To associate means to find a picture which may not *strictly* connect with the scene but, my goodness, how it connects *psychologically*. For example, the psychology of the railway station and the psychology of Mary sitting alone in the house with Cathleen and really confessing something to her.

We know that Mary is high. She uses drugs. It is obvious she doesn't want to be alone. She wants to escape from loneliness. She is in the house with only her servant. And this doesn't happen very often; usually she is observed. It is a moment in which she feels safe. No one is watching her, and she wants to talk to someone, right? What is another situation of a human being that I can compare with this—of being safely alone and needing to talk to someone?

'It could be a waitress,' Elizabeth suggested. 'Waitresses sometimes want to talk and don't have time and go back in circles to their tables.'

'Yes, Elizabeth, but it is not right. It will not meet their situation,' observed Cynkutis.

'Well, a lot of people talk when they're getting a haircut,' Jackie said. 'Hairdressers know that and when people come to get a haircut, they spend a lot of their time listening.'

Bravo, Jackie! That is a very good association and incredibly powerful, because it provides you and your partner with a certain opportunity to improvise. So in this case, the actress playing

Cathleen will be like a hairdresser. And she should not be afraid even to wash your hair and work with your hair and during all this you are talking to her. You will improvise the scene like that, and because in the play it is not really the situation of being at the hairdresser you will find that some things click and some don't. But what *does click* your senses will remember; your imagination will be attacked by this.

Later, you will exclude the circumstances that make the association obvious, but you and Cathleen, in this living room will know that for you, it is like the situation of being at the hairdressers. And maybe Cathleen will touch your hair or maybe you will touch her hair. And maybe you will be all the time talking to Cathleen over your shoulder as though she is behind you doing your hair. You will never talk to her facing her directly but will always talk with her like that. It will be something very important, how this relationship is built.

So you see, you associated. But why did you associate? Because I took this seed intellectually, this seed from the scene. I excluded a lot of things. I said, 'She is alone in the house, safely alone and she needs to talk with someone.' I then asked, 'What other situation is alive in this?'

The way to associate is to eliminate from the scene which you are analysing everything that is not essential. To try as deeply as possible to capture what is essential in what you feel. Even if you think you may be making a mistake, don't be afraid to associate with another picture, with another situation. Because you need to try each association, and if it is not right, it will show you that mistake. But you need to try.

'So we have to find the person's main intention?' Judith asked.

'It can be the intention or not,' Cynkutis replied. 'Because what we are doing now, we are not talking at all about the intention of Mary.'

'But you said she needs to talk to someone,' Judith persisted. 'Well, I guess that's not an intention either; she doesn't know she needs to talk to someone.'

'Yes, she does,' said Jackie. 'She keeps saying, 'Stay with me.' She doesn't want to be alone.'

'This search for intention is a very dangerous question,' Cynkutis warned us. 'In life, we are doing a lot of things, and we don't know our intentions. That's why the dramaturgy of life is so dramatic. If we know everything, if we know our intentions, I think it will be absolutely boring because I will exclude everything that is not in my intention.'

'But if you know the role, that's what you do. You search for the intentions in the play,' Elizabeth insisted.

'Petit bourgeois mentality in the theatre for the petit bourgeois,' he scoffed.

'God! That's what I studied all last year!' Elizabeth exclaimed.

'What if you worked out the association like Jackie just did and researched that?' said Judith. 'And, while you were experimenting, you found out that your intention was exactly that: you don't want to be alone. I guess you're just saying you can't experience it?'

Cynkutis quickly clarified: 'No, that is not what I am saying. With what *you* experience, with the intentions of the actress playing Mary, I am with you, because your intentions for me are important. But for me, the intentions of Mary are not important.'

'But a lot of teachers teach you to think that way,' continued Judith. 'What does the character want to do? But I guess, if you work that way, it means you have it all sewed up in a nice little package and that's not giving you any room to explore.'

'Exactly . . . exactly. Then you are *creating* the intention of Mary,' Cynkutis agreed.

'In that case,' Judith said, 'I'm marking the intention ahead of time. But, if I work through association, I'll have some choices and then I can decide what the intention is?'

‘Exactly,’ he said. ‘If you find the intention of Mary by analysing and asking, “What is her real intention?”, it is a paper character and you will never be able to feel it.’

‘I find it by investigating myself and then I decide?’ asked Judith.

‘You find it through the association.’

‘If you have a wrong association, if you think something and you do it and it’s the wrong association, it won’t work for you. What do you do then?’ I asked. ‘Do you just try a different association?’

‘Exactly.’

The concept was beginning to make sense, but I had one more question: ‘If the director has an overall concept of the image for the piece and then, within the separate scenes, there are smaller environments that create what you’re working on, how do things fit together? It seems like one association is almost enough to go through a play.’

Cynkutis continued to clarify:

> Oh no. It seems to be, but it is not. In ordinary, common life there is a certain logic, but for the theatre, there is another kind of logic which is artistic. For instance, in common life we name someone logical if their actions are consequential. If the person is going from point A to point B and point B is supported by A and that’s why he is then continuing on to C and from C to B. He is not jumping; his actions are consequences. These are the kind of people about whom we can say, ‘Oh, it’s clear to see his past and it is easy to say what will be in his future.’ We see where he is going. His character is logical.
>
> But we are pulled in many directions by everything in our life. Not only pulled by experiences, but also by emotions and feelings. And we can be like children: we can cry with great pain and sorrow, and then one second later we can laugh. And this does not mean that you are crazy. Because what joins these two attitudes, or these two parts, is *you*. It is you.

> We are permanently full of very different feelings and emotions, and what joins them is *me*. Only *I* can be witness to myself. Only *I* can understand or not understand—which is also good—what is going on in me. If it is very important, I will try to understand. If it is not essentially important, I will ignore it and just feel what is going on. If someone is trying to create a character on the stage that has only one expression and everything is on that same line from the beginning to the end, it is poor acting.

'But how will the audience know that it's the same character if the role is not consistent?' I persisted.

Cynkutis exploded with mock scolding and delight:

> Consistency is for petit bourgeois theatre! You must keep your curiosity alive! In each act or in each scene you can develop something that will provide you, as an actor, with spontaneity and impulses to act. And even if you do not feel the logic between the first scene and the second scene, it is logical as long as you are doing it spontaneously. Because you, as an actor, are the spinal cord of the character. Whatever you do, if you do it spontaneously, if you do it with your self-confidence, if you trust what you are doing, it is only enriching the part.
>
> So if you can make a conclusion from these views: to associate is not only to compare one reality with another but actively to check it. Because real association happens by work. It is not only an intellectual process; it is active investigation. And, if you give yourself time to investigate, if it is right, it provides you with unexpected possibilities. Many won't work and can be like mistakes. And when you worked, there were a lot of things that were not mistakes, but they were not so interesting. For instance, the very first time, Jackie, when you started to say the text, it was a kind of performance that you did. Do you remember what I am talking about?

'Yes.'

'But later you started again and my goodness, it was not a performance! At the very end, when you started to talk to Diane, it was absolutely full,' he asserted.

'The first time, I felt my body language more neurotically,' Jackie admitted.

> OK, but it was exactly the same with Elizabeth. The very first time she started, it was almost empty. But she didn't give up because she saw that you were not giving up. She was inspired by you and, later on, she inspired you when she joined you. The very first time Judith started, it was well done. Let's say it was on a good average level of acting done by her. But later, Judith, when you started to speak, something very different appeared. The very first time you started, it was with certain mannerisms you have. With this movement . . .
>
> [*He demonstrated.*]
>
> OK? But, later, you took something from the others, and you joined with them. Taking relaxation in your movement and in your voice.
>
> The very first time David started, it was intense but not very interesting. But he made it. It was made by him. Later, David, you went on the chair and when you started to talk in the third person, my goodness, it was very powerful. And it was something really very sharp.
>
> You see it is important that when you rehearse, you feel the freedom to make mistakes. You have the right to make mistakes. I cannot imagine the development of something on the stage without mistakes. If there are no mistakes something is wrong. It means the actors don't risk anything, and they are using only what they know. It means they are conserving something. Conserving something like their own achievements. I know that

their abilities are bigger, and they are not showing me their real abilities. Usually, in this case, I am trying to make a revolution, making everything upside down, crashing their logic and security and asking them to make mistakes. Please make mistakes. Make mistakes, have fun. Well, we will meet again at five.

CHAPTER SEVENTEEN

# ANIMATION

## Saturday, 23 June 1984: Evening Session in the Loft

*Theatre without changing the workshop of an actor cannot change.*

This evening, Cynkutis asked us to begin by using the plastiques to explore different parts of the body, to 'dialogue' with each other and with objects in the space. He then continued with this morning's exercise of embodying emotions. We started by walking briskly and, as we walked, Cynkutis called out, 'Sadness! Jealousy! Surprise! Anger!' continually increasing the tempo and urgency of the exercise until we were responding quickly in the moment.

## Animation

### *Preparation for Animation*

Cynkutis directed us to the next task:

> Take a chair and place it at a distance from the others. Begin by sitting in your chair and then walk towards another person with the intention of sitting in their chair. The person who is seated will leave their chair at the last possible moment to make way for you. Remember, if you are seated and see someone approaching, remain seated. Do not leave your chair until you must, and do not touch! Do not interrupt or stop the other's movement—only change positions.

This dynamic exercise brought us into immediate relationship. As always, Cynkutis' presence and the complete attention he brought when he watched our work helped us to bring our whole selves to the task.

'Perform the task faster,' he urged. 'Perform the task as fast as you can!'

We were consumed by trying to execute the task as precisely as possible. The energy from each person's work fed the other's and soon we were bathed in sweat.

Cynkutis called from the side, 'Now, when you approach a person who is sitting, whenever you can, work in pairs. Join with another for this action of taking their chair.'

Being part of a duo was powerful and strong. The configuration naturally created a situation of power and intimidation as we vanquished one lone person or were ourselves displaced by the approach of a united team. It was clear that this exercise, rooted in the body's organic experience, had created intense personal dynamics between us.

Without giving us time to rest or write down our experiences, Cynkutis marshalled our energy and drove us forward: 'Leave your chairs and walk quickly in the middle of the space. Pass each other and come as close as you can without touching. Feel warmth in your chest area. Energy is coming from the middle of your chest. Give this energy to another, chest to chest.'

Energized by the earlier work, we moved dynamically around each other, looking for a way to make this happen. Initially, exchanging energy through the chest seemed like an abstract idea, but gradually—as though engaging a muscle that is almost never used—I began to feel a heightening of sensation in the chest, as though possibly, just possibly, something was there.

Cynkutis' investment in the process was continuous and absolute: 'Come as close as you can but do not touch. Move quickly and change direction when you are not exchanging energy with someone else. Continue finding new partners,' he coached.

We were in constant motion.

*Animation*

Cynkutis left his chair along the outer edge of the workspace and entered the exercise. I could see him peripherally, moving among the others until finally he came over to work with me. My whole focus was on giving him energy from my chest area, working so hard it felt as though the energy was going out through the top of my head as well.

My efforts to constantly give left no room to receive and prevented me from being easily able to sense what Cynkutis was doing. But when he came ever closer, when he was about two feet away and facing me, I suddenly felt the force that was coming from him. I experienced it as a warm vibration, a presence at the top of my head. Then, suddenly, his energy overcame mine entering me through the crown of my head making its way down what felt like the inner column of my body, moving, spiralling steadily down, through the core of my self, subtly mixing energy with my own until some kind of base was reached in the lowest area of my spinal column. At that point, the current rebounded off my pelvic floor, and a silvery river of energy was released in me—or perhaps I was released into it—it was hard to know which. Until the moment when my energy was animated, I hadn't noticed if anyone else was in a special state. But when I entered the experience, it became clear that Cynkutis had activated something inside each of us, somehow releasing an energetic source, giving us an altered experience of ourselves as well as the environment, creating a living pool of energy in the space. It was experiential and undeniable. I was absorbed by the presence of this energy, merged with and supported by it. It was in and all around me like a delicious magnetic fluid that transfixed and transformed everything.

Cynkutis was in constant motion, completely given to the task. His breathing was deep and laboured from the exertion, but he spoke to us, keeping us oriented towards his original instructions: 'Continue with the task, exchanging energy with each other from the chest.'

As we continued, approaching each other and giving each other energy from the chest, it became apparent that the way in which each person participated was quite different. It was as though our core personas were revealing themselves in this new environment.

Judith's energy was directed in its focus like a clear, intense channel. Jackie was steady and measured as she moved from one to another. David's eyes were shining, his movements were soft and fluid and he seemed suffused with love. For my part, I became aware of a stoic aspect to my energetic exchange. My tendency was only to give and not to easily receive. But when I encountered Elizabeth in this communal pool, it was a shock. She was on a hunt for energy, and when she found the stream that I was producing, she stayed near me making manic 'eating' gestures—grabbing with her hands and making motions into her mouth as though she were gobbling up the energy. I was able to disengage from her but observed her acting the same way with others, feeding herself in what seemed a demonic manner. It was definitely disturbing though, as we continued, individual differences in approach began to vanish.

The energy in the room rose until it seemed to pass a certain threshold. The atmosphere around us now felt full. It was as though we were completely surrounded and supported by a loving energy and I, along with the others, was dancing in it, afloat and swimming in it, like some strange, charged fluid.

Cynkutis indicated that generating energy from the chest was no longer necessary and drew us into an improvisational framework in which we sang and danced in this boundless, beautiful energy. To this day, I marvel at the old audio files from that evening and the sound of our strange, ethereal singing, filled with overtones.

As this ecstatic experience unfolded, Cynkutis began to lead us in a circular dance around a central point. An improvisation evolved in which we were a tribe dancing around a central fire. At last, Cynkutis repeatedly hunched his body downwards, bringing his hands lower towards the ground as though with this movement and rhythm he was containing and quelling the fire. The circle grew tighter as we grouped closer around him, bending and lowering our own hands, bit by bit quieting the flames. As our image of the central fire ebbed ever lower, the energy of our improvisation died down too until, at last, our palms were flat on the wooden floor and the fire had become ashes. The event was over and the magical energy we had just experienced was returned to the ground.

Cynkutis' face was red and he was breathing rapidly as though from great athletic exertion. I looked around at the members of our group. Their eyes were shining with wonder at what had just taken place. David's eyes were filled with adoration as he looked at Cynkutis. For my part, I felt calm and objective even though what I had just experienced was unlike anything I had ever thought possible and felt nothing short of miraculous.

Cynkutis looked around at the group. He obviously didn't think the worshipful looks he was seeing were good for anyone because he immediately countered it with practical words that deflated the awe we felt, grounding the experience:

> What we have done, this energy, the ability to contact this energy, is not magic or God or religion; it is a human capacity a human ability. In a few minutes we will speak more, but now take time to rest for several moments. You can stay here or walk outside. We will meet again in fifteen minutes.

It was hard to leave this gathering, this moment in time, even hard to stand-up. It had been an extreme yet intimate experience and each of us felt gentle towards the others. I remember exchanging a smile with Judith, acknowledging that we had just shared something unbelievable. Some of us stayed indoors lying on the floor, others went outside so they could be in nature. For once, I didn't feel like writing in my notebook.

## Conversation: Paratheatre and Animation[1]

When we gathered again, Cynkutis was composed and relaxed, but Judith was full of questions: 'Does this—what just happened—does this happen at Laboratory Theatre performances?' We leaned forward, trying not to miss a word. David almost dropped his recorder while quickly pulling it out from his pocket. Cynkutis' response was quiet but measured:

> **[Audio #11]** All together we know a lot about it. When we are working together, we know how to switch it. That's why we stopped performing because it was so easy. We were able to almost always switch on such a process.

'So why did you stop performing?' asked Judith.

> Because it was like keeping it for our own selves and not sharing it with others. That's why we decided to speak and to teach. And it is exciting how you can evoke such an energy. I, by myself, as you saw, I was able to evoke this energy among you five, together with myself. If I will be with some of my friends in the company, we can do it for twenty at once. Three of us, we can do it for twenty-seven. If there are four of us, we can do it for thirty-five. When there was six of us, we were able to do it for fifty. When we were seven, we were able to do it for sixty-five people. When we did it in January '79, the *Tree of People* project, we did it for sixty-five people from different countries, and it was seven days and seven nights non-stop.
>
> Because if we are five [Laboratory Theatre actors], we do depend on ourselves; but if there is a bigger number of people, there is a lot of surprises. Always someone is coming with something. If you start to sing a song, it is almost sure that after a few

1 Cynkutis used the verb 'to animate' to describe the transmission and activation of these energies. But it is my decision, as the author, to use it more broadly in the text to describe when this process was being activated. It was also my choice to use it as a noun: 'animation'.

minutes, after silence, someone else will start a song, and someone else will join. When it will be done, probably someone else will start to dance. And, at the same time, some people who are very tired will fall asleep on the floor, without going somewhere else, and they will sleep, and other people will take care of them, covering them by blankets so they will not get cold, and this care is another source of energy. So when they are waking up, they see around themselves activity and they are from one world joining another world, and they are bringing something else. It starts, really, another chain in the process.

'When you eat or how you ate . . . you ate during the process?' Elizabeth asked.

> Oh sure . . . because in this huge room [area] in which there are three floors, in the corridor there is one big bar with juices, with milk, with hot tea. Because there is a group of people who are all the time taking care of those who are working. Those who at the moment are tired, for instance, but they are not going to sleep—they are going to serve food for those who can come to eat. So there is always a hot meal or hot coffee and, one time a day, a very hot, real dinner.

'What caused an ending?' Judith queried softly.

> You know, nothing, really. The moment in which the energy was stopped, it was over. And it didn't happen at once. Someone stopped after three days. Someone stopped after three days and four nights. Someone stopped after the fifth day. But they stayed. The only problem was that they didn't feel able enough to join but they didn't want to leave. So they were around because we had rooms in which people were able to read and to sleep and all the time they listened to this activity from rooms. Because it was almost permanently sounds and music, never mechanical music, sounds or music from voices, from bodies.

When everyone was almost . . . like waves, it was quiet; it was done. It was evident. Like fire has flame and later ashes. It is done.

The very first time was for seven days and seven nights, but we were not able to provide people later with such long experiences because we had other duties also. So later we made it for three days and two nights. Usually, thirty-five or forty people were coming from different parts of Poland, from different parts of Europe, from United States. You never knew who you would meet.

'Are you going to do it again at all maybe?' Jackie interjected.

'No, the company disbands. I am going back to teach everything again and to start again. But, who knows?' he said leaving the possibility in the air.

'There's only four of you left now?' Elizabeth asked.

'Now we are only four alive: Zygmunt Molik, Ryszard Cieślak, Rena Mirecka, and I from those days.'[2]

'Wasn't there Kozłowski?' Jackie queried.

'[Zbigniew] Kozłowski, but he is from the young company, he is the second company which came very late, in the 70s. They never reached this secret which was necessary to do it.'

'Did you work in equal time indoors and outdoors or did you mostly work outdoors?' asked Judith.

---

2 It is unclear why Cynkutis does not mention Mieczysław Janowski, an important part of the company for eight years, or Maja Komorowska, or Elizabeth Albahaca. Perhaps it is because the events Cynkutis is referring to happened during the time of paratheatre and beyond and these actors had left the company by that time. Komorowska left in 1968, Janowski in 1970.

No, we mostly worked indoors. We were in the city.

We got our farm[3] and we got our possibilities much later. In 1971, we got an environment to investigate everything outside. So the paratheatrical work starts from 1971, but it was already channelled and stimulated by theatrical achievement. We knew that if we want to go forward, we had to jump from the stage and to go back to nature.

Since 1971, mainly, we were looking for people who want just to come without any specific needs. We were looking at how to *not* organize the time only to have everything that is necessary to be in a place as long as possible. And a lot of knowledge came from these experiences. Later we learned how to organize time and to not kill this spontaneous possibility which people are bringing.

But, for instance, when only we met, we from the group, it never happened. Because each of us is very armed. We know too much. And even if we don't know, we sometimes do manipulate. We know when something starts for instance. Someone who is from the outside is not even conscious that at that moment something clicked. But we know something clicked in the moment among energies of people. Something already starts. No one knows. But we know. Something already starts and when we know that something already starts we know how to use it. So we, with our knowledge, we can help, but we can destroy also everything. **[End Audio #11]** Come, let us continue our work.

---

3 Cynkutis is referring to their base at Brzezinka, near Oleśnica, where, beginning in 1971, much of the paratheatrical experimentation took place. It still remains the 'forest base' for the activities of the Grotowski Institute in Wrocław.

### Text and Energy Exchange with Partners

> Take your chairs and place them opposite a partner. Whether you stand or sit is not important, but face them and feel warm energy in your chest. Send this energy, create energy, in the middle of the space between you. When something has begun between you, move out into this central area and exchange energy with each other. Come close, but do not touch each other. Feel warmth between you, this energy that keeps you united. When you hear me ask you to change partners, move to another chair and find a new partner.

Our awareness of the unusual energies that could arise in the work lent a searching, almost desperate quality to our attempts. After several minutes, Cynkutis stopped us and spoke of the vectors involved:

> In these two experiences that began this work: first, a warm area in the chest and exchanging energy, later this contact between and among you, awareness of body-to-body and, through the body, something else: giving energy, and drinking from that energy and feeding from the energy—in each of those experiences there are vectors. This first vector: *towards, towards, towards* someone else is very important. The second vector was 'do not touch the other person', 'take care', or 'do not lose this warm area'.
>
> Let us again establish opposing vectors clearly in the body. Take a chair and put it in front of you. Push against this chair with your body but do not allow the chair to move. Your body must create two vectors; one to move the chair and one that holds everything back.

Intense and physical, this work brought a dull ache to my solar plexus. Was this exercise, like the Cat, designed to awaken energy centres in the body? The drone of a large tractor mowing the grass outside seemed to come from some distant, unreal place.

Cynkutis continued to develop the exercise:

> Now, as we did a few days ago, sit on your chair in such a way that you will begin to relate your body to the chair. At that time, I showed you how to take, somehow, the form of an object into your body.[4] Take the chair into your body as one vector. The second vector will be the exchange of energy with your partner using lines of text from the first scene between Tyrone and Mary. Diane and Jackie, you will work first. Please bring your chairs and place them at a distance from each other.

He indicated that our chairs should be about fifteen feet apart.

> Stand, please, behind your chairs. Take for yourself a few sentences from this scene. They can be in any order and can be repeated many times. Feel the presence of your partner first, then use your text to send energy to move your partner. Affect your partner with your text.

I gripped the back of my chair with both hands taking the chair's unyielding planes into my body. I felt rooted as though the chair were some kind of magnetic pole, an incredibly strong vector against which I could work. I faced Jackie and squirmed my body down, trying to find the source of the text or the root of some sound. Jackie spoke first. She seemed defenceless as she faced me, only lightly holding on to her chair. I responded by trying to move her with my text as Cynkutis had instructed, trying as hard as I could to 'do something to my partner'. At the very least, I wanted her to receive energy from me.

I noticed that as the exchange continued, Jackie seemed to be trying to avoid me, to physically move out of the way. At one point, she even ducked behind her chair, but I was relentless in my efforts. Then a strange thing happened. As I was directing text and energy towards her, Jackie suddenly walked sideways in a staccato, mechanical way, a jerky

---

4 See the section 'Sourcing Objects and Others Using Vectors' in Chapter 5 (pp. 42–43).

automaton pattern that clearly was not initiated by her. I wasn't sure what was happening, but I felt that my energy had somehow controlled her for a moment, trapped her in a kind of energy field and, involuntarily and against her will, she was forced to move. She tried to avoid me even more now and there was panic and desperation in her movements.

After I had seen those first strange movements, I tried even harder to influence her and succeeded one more time in moving her in a jerky pattern. The movements were not natural at all. It looked as though she were controlled by some external magnetic force. After several more minutes, Cynkutis ended the improvisation and asked Jackie and David to begin work.

I sat to the side, feeling stunned. What had just happened between me and Jackie? Why had Jackie moved in that strange, inhuman way? I had no answers, only questions.

Jackie and David's improvisation and then Judith and David's all proceeded normally, although the energy work we'd done before gave the exchanges an intense focus. Judith's approach contrasted with the seriousness of everyone else's. She was playful and light, almost funny, adroitly dodging and disarming each text David lobbed her way.

Then Cynkutis paired me with Elizabeth. I approached the task the same way I had with Jackie, with intensity and ferocity.

Elizabeth was focused on me and seemed much stronger than before. The investment of energy from the previous exercises was like a deep reservoir everyone was drinking from. We both gripped our chairs as we began the text exchange and then suddenly both of us began to exactly mirror each other's movements. We both walked in small, rapid, jerky steps doing everything precisely the same. Matching each other exactly. These involuntary, mechanical movements seemed similar to the motion that magnets make when two positive poles are pressed against each other. The strange, fast, repetitive, matching movements happened one more time during our text exchange, though it was impossible to say what was triggering it. At last, Cynkutis brought the improvisation to a close with 'Thank you for your work.' As we rested, he spoke about what he had witnessed. Clearly excited, his voice echoed in the resonant space:

> **[Audio #12]** It was evident that in this [first] improvisation between you [Jackie and Diane] there was a relationship like snake and fly. She [Diane] was like a snake, all the time preparing to capture. It is why, you [Jackie] wanted to change her energy, because she was too active for you, and you were trying to stop her. I knew you wanted to stop her and to push her to the situation in which she will receive energy from you because, otherwise, you were all the time receiving energy from her. I knew it, but I didn't stop, because it was already providing me with an idea—how incredible—the relationship of Tyrone and Mary is like snake and fly! And, in a human sense, watch how it fits! Mary from the beginning is 'prey'. She has no chance to win, right?

The group agreed and Cynkutis continued to develop his ideas.

'She has no chance to win. She must lose everything because he is such a snake and because she is in the position of a fly,' Cynkutis reasoned.

'But I think she almost creates that herself,' Elizabeth interposed. 'She's beside herself and has no control.'

'Exactly,' he said, 'that's why she's using drugs!'

'You know what I thought when I was watching that?' said Judith. 'That this fly also has weapons, a stinger, like a bee or a wasp, because the use of drugs has to sting Tyrone. I mean, I could be wrong. She could be totally helpless, totally a victim.'

'OK, but watch!', said Cynkutis. 'Already you had something; I had something; there was something alive! Something that we can use to create this relationship, and we are using it for investigation: how to make, you know, realistic sense.'

Cynkutis turned to David, to explore what he had seen in his work with Judith:

When you [David] started your work with Judith. It was after a few minutes, you thought, 'That's not fair from Judith' [what she was doing]. You were focusing how to create this magnetic, this energetic pool.[5] And, after a few minutes, it was absolutely obvious that she is like kitten, and he is like a dog. Or he is like cat, and she is like mouse. It was absolutely a good proposition in which he is like a hunter and she doesn't know that she is playing with danger. She was able to come closer, but he had his claws [to strike]. Very obvious. So it is already another variation how we search.

When you [Diane and Elizabeth] started too, after a few minutes, it was evident that we had another possibility: two puppets. Someone animates them, too. She [Diane] doesn't know that she is animated and she [Elizabeth] doesn't know that she is animated. Two puppets. Two human puppets on stage. A tragic situation, you know? And again, if you will read this scene, we can find that they are like two puppets. This means that, [through these improvisations], we provide ourselves with conclusions or with stimulation, artistic stimulation, without intellectual masturbation. We are getting it from work.

If we will select which form we like best, ['Cat and Mouse' or 'Two Puppets' or 'Snake and Fly'] you already know how to start playing it because it is rooted in your activities. You showed certain abilities. It is not like saying, 'Judith, I would like you to play Mary,' and Judith is saying, 'Me? Why?' You know why. Because there is something coming from you already in this proposal. You understand what I mean?

---

5 Cynkutis is referring to David's frustration with the playfulness of Judith's approach. She didn't respond to anything seriously, including the pool of magnetic energy he was trying to create with her. Because of this, he changed his tactics to more of an attack.

It is not like the director who is coming to the theatre with his idea and is thinking 'Oh, my Mary must have grey hair . . . ' and is watching for an actress who looks like his image. No! The idea is that the director is spending, for instance, five or six hours working with actors and making such tasks, giving them a chance to improvise. And, among those who are [improvising], it is evident that one, at the moment, is bringing the most exciting possibility for Mary. Something that he didn't even expect can be done. That's why, for him, it is a surprise. For the actress who is doing it, it is also a surprise. The director is extremely curious about the abilities of the actress because it is something that he is already able to grab from her. So he is working much better with the actress, not manipulating the actress, but trying, from the actress, to grab as much as possible.

It is quite a different relationship in work, not only on the stage, but in the work it is different. The director is really working for the actor because from the actor he is trying to get as much as possible. And the actor is giving as much as possible for the director because [he or she] believes the director is providing them with circumstances in which [their] abilities and talent can come out. **[End Audio #12]**

But let us come back to what we did today because the time is coming to be very late. Today I did ask you to explore certain tasks and, along the way, we did encounter a different source of energy.

**[Audio #13]** This energy is in our body. We can bring it. Because it is not something that just can happen accidentally by acting and saying the text and sitting, moving or creating a situation. It needs something else. It is a certain life, presence. It is impossible to create this life or to open this life using old-fashioned stage development. Impossible.

If someone is thinking that we are at the end of the twentieth century, still making copies of bourgeois theatre from the nineteenth century, and if someone is trying to change it by making new designs or new lights or new costumes—instead of using wool for making dresses using plastic or plexiglass or whatever—it still is the same bullshit as it was only with a new design. Because theatre without changing the workshop of an actor cannot change.

The actor who will not discover new forms and new abilities to explore their own organism—their own feelings, own emotions, own body, and own expressions—if someone is not providing the actor with such possibilities for exploration usually the actor is falling back on everything that is known. It is like a snake that is biting its own tail. A lot of ideas about making new theatre, but still, everything is kept the same.

Definitely [we need to make] such an investigation, definitely exploration with no fear—looking at how to open more and more your artistic, human sources to bring into the light something that is never used. It is the way to find how we can really change a lot of things. How we can go really very far.

All the time, everything that we are doing is not accidental because everything as you see has a certain structure. I am asking you first to build a certain structure and later you improvise on this structure. Like, for instance, today I gave you the sense of this energy, and later you did investigate using this structure. Well, it looks like a structure, but it is not. But you know something! You have this feeling: 'We know something.' However, it is not that we know, but we have this feeling that's inside during the process. That's why a lot of things can happen. Thank you. See you tomorrow. **[End Audio #13]**

CHAPTER EIGHTEEN

# IMPROVISATIONS

## Sunday, 24 June 1984: Daytime Session in the Theatre

*Improvise on the basis of knowledge—never without knowledge.*

### Improvising Using an 'Attacking' Energy

Cynkutis began our session with a group exercise:

> Today we will continue our work from yesterday. Gather in the middle of the space and walk quickly. Move around each other and bring your bodies as close as you can without touching. Sometimes encounter each other facing chest to chest, but also sometimes avoid this. In the area of the chest, when you are facing someone else, find the energy that wants to attack. Exchange that energy.

For twenty exhausting minutes, we worked in this way. Calling up this kind of energy was intense and almost impossible to sustain. I kept trying to find a source for it so that I would have something to drink from, but I was not successful. It seemed odd to be manufacturing this aggressive energy from the chest. I think of attack as being a strong impulse from shoulders, knees, and head. Isn't the chest area related to love and the heart? Still I kept trying, ratcheting up my energy for the attack and then watching it spiral quickly down. In my partner work the previous day, I had been able to sustain something like an attacking energy, but the text had helped me to engage and I had also relied heavily on the chair as a grounding second vector.

Cynkutis then incorporated our energy work into a scene:

> In this improvisation I want you to use this attacking energy as one of your tools. The situation is: there has been a death in the family and the money, the inheritance, is going to be divided. Each of you wants your share, and each of you feels that your share should be more than anyone else's. Set up the space, the room where you will gather. Use your text from *Long Day's Journey into Night.*

With boxes, we created a room-like structure that we could enter and leave. At one end, we placed a desk with a semi-circle of chairs facing it. The environment we created and Cynkutis' clear proposal helped me. I began to prowl around the furniture, discovering with my body a crouching, secretive persona that combined animosity and stealth. The only problem was that I couldn't sustain what I was working with. Once an impulse or action was finished, my energy drained quickly away. Then, Cynkutis gave us more tools to solve this very problem.

## Improvising with Props

After stopping our scene work, Cynkutis directed us over to where a number of potential props were stored: 'It is important to select the right prop as an additional source for the work. Let's see how it can be to work with an object.'[1]

---

1 Richard Mennen described how important object work was to Cynkutis: 'Particularly the animation [ . . . ] of an object: so that the object had its own life. [ . . . ] that life inspired your [scenic] life' (in Dunkelberg 2008: 527). Mennen also reflected on their use in Cynkutis' *DOOR* project in Pittsburgh:

> Out of this rehearsal and training process a central metaphoric object emerged: They worked around a door. We got a big door, and the title of it became *DOOR*. Two people carrying this door. The door became various things: their cross, something that they entered through, a table, a bed. It just went through all these different transformations. [ . . . ] Zbyszek

Although we had worked with set pieces and props before, this time Cynkutis improvised using a plate as his prop, continually changing his relationship to it. Never did he interact with it as a known entity—a simple surface on which food is served—and because it wasn't treated literally, the object became metaphorical, many-levelled and fluid. Even more interesting, the physical presence of the object produced a grounding of the energy, a vector that brought with it a special concentration and force.

'Now, find the object you will bring with you into this improvisation. It can be from this prop table or from objects you have with you today,' he instructed.

One person brought a sheaf of papers. I found a pen and as I held it, I realized I was gripping a knife. We began the improvisation and once again this work unleashed a primal stream of impulses in me. I felt like a predator and could clearly sense the weak energy in those around me. There was something lacklustre in their investment in this struggle. Could *they* possibly win this prize, this fortune? How easy it would be to take it from them! Jackie and Judith began using their texts in a heady way as though they were part of a legal argument, but I was not going to join them in some intellectual world.

I lunged forward towards the desk of papers, capturing it. Taking the surfaces of the desk and its steel-like quality into my body, I guarded the papers, keeping the others at bay using my text. I used the pen to caress and covet the pages, all the while keeping an eye on the others. I had clearly dropped even the facade of politeness. Cynkutis' continued emphasis on commitment to the task had made me bold.

Jackie jumped back as I attacked the pile of papers. The others also backed off. They would be no match for me unless they reached this

---

was very interested in the American thing, so there was kind of an American theme to it: something to do with freedom, something to do with commercialism [ . . . ]. (In Dunkelberg 2008: 527–28)

intensity. As I faced them, I felt a ripple in their communal energy. They had sensed the power in their numbers and were gathering against me, coming towards me slowly as a group. Using their texts, they tried to get me to move away from the papers, but I held my ground. Finally, Cynkutis called an end to the improvisation, not with a clear resolution but as a stand-off.

He commented:

> It is amazing how specific objects do affect us, and they can become such a source that they do stimulate strong associations every time. When we were touring *Apocalypsis* in Paris, we brought with us from Poland even the lighting instruments we used to develop the work. We were tuned at such a level that those same lights were essential for us to respond fully—organically.[2]

## Conversation: The Actor as Artist

'What do you think of the acting profession here?' Judith asked. 'How does it differ from work in Europe or Poland or elsewhere?'

Cynkutis raised one eyebrow and looked at us askance to indicate the many problems he saw before responding:

> I think that something is definitely wrong in the way the acting profession is treated in your country. Even if you look at the hierarchy in the theatre here, you will find that in the very top place is the producer, in the second place is the director and author, in the third place is the assistant of the director or the assistant of the producer, later will be the designer, later the assistant of the designer, later will be—who else—the master who is doing

2 Mennen's account of helping Cynkutis find a loaf of bread to use as a prop in the US performances of *Apocalypsis cum Figuris* is an example of how precise the Laboratory Theatre actors were about the stimulation provided by concrete objects (in Cynkutis 2015a: 28–29).

> the lighting and others. At the very bottom is the actor and 'shop!'

He laughed, delighted at his depiction of theatre in the US.

> So, if your structure is like that, it represents exactly how high or how low is acting in this scale of theatre. I think this problem is because art is not supported here; the state is not giving money for culture. If theatre is not protected by the state, it comes to be like it is in the United States—a product. When culture is lower, habits are lower. When habits are lower, the relationship among people is lower. It is a slow process, but it reflects on the life of the common people. It is really a question of what we are doing and why we are doing it. It is also my question.
>
> It was always, from the beginning of the theatre, that someone powerful and rich was protecting theatre, like the king had his clown and court theatre. If it is not like that, then you have human vultures, like managers, who are buying actors and selling actors. They are talking that they are taking care of your development, maybe some of them really do, but mainly they don't. They want to sell you. And many of your actors want to be sold.
>
> We have, in our country, people who we know are good actors, and we respect them. But none of these actors who are respected are showing their buttocks to sell a new kind of vodka or spaghetti. That kind of work can be done by someone else, not an actor.

'What's the proper hierarchy in the theatre?' Judith asked.

Cynkutis responded easily: In the first place is the actor and director, in the second is the author. He continued:

> But, as an actor, to be named an *artist* it is necessary to share something on a very high level and show certain skills on a very high level. It is also a problem of material and time in which

these skills can really vibrate to create art. I respect the calling to be an actor very much, and I know that, even if I am keeping my skills as high as possible, that is not enough to make me an artist.

**[Audio #14]** The moment of art is like a moment of meeting with certain strengths and devotion and a certain vocation, a call. It is a moment in which something *through me* shows me what to do and speaks to me what to select. It is not usually what I can plan or what I can schedule. I keep myself ready for such a moment so that when it will come, I will be ready to take this duty, I will be ready to answer by my voice, by my body, by my health. But it comes from time to time and goes away. Only when it comes, when I feel I am responding and something speaks through me in such a way, I am very happy. And I know in this moment the artist is in me. But at the same time, I know that when it will be done it will go away and I will be a craftsman, just a craftsman: someone who knows how to keep their skills and how to work and how to wait again for such a meeting with something that would like through me to speak. It is a service.

Mainly I am not an artist, mainly I am a craftsman. And I try to make my craft as high as possible, to develop more and more about the craft, to find different keys, how to concentrate my energy, how, in each moment of my life, when my body is getting older and older, to drink from each page new possibilities, because each page is opening at the same time new possibilities which I didn't expect even when I was young.

So I try to be up to date with the time. The time of my life and the time of life around me. I keep my skills. I want to know what is going on around the world.

Cynkutis spoke with certainty and commitment:

And if there is something that I do not understand, I don't give up. I try to work to understand. So, it is how to be ready. I am

> not going to be a politician or physician, but I want to know a lot about medicine and a lot about politics. I am doing it for the stage, for people with whom I make theatre, and for myself. I don't want to be isolated. I don't want to be cut off from information or cut off from other cultures.
>
> If someone is talking to me about ghosts, I want to know what a ghost is; I don't ignore the possibility that ghosts exist. If someone is talking to me about God, I want to understand God. And I don't doubt that God exists because it is only a different name for something that I do believe, too. **[End Audio #14]**

We were all quiet, moved by his deep commitment, hoping we would be able to hold on to the artistic ideal he had just evoked in us.

Cynkutis broke the silence, 'Come onto the stage again, please, for the next task.'

## Improvising Using Animal Associations

As always, Cynkutis' voice was present and alive as he outlined the task: 'Find an animal you can associate with the character you found in the previous improvisation. Then we will again work with this same scene. You may repeat some elements from before; however, it is not necessary to do everything exactly as it was.'

I reflected on the character I had found. The attacking energy had been in my head and jaw and my movements reminded me of a dog defending its territory. But then I sensed that something wilder lay underneath and realized the association of 'wolf' fit better.

Repeating something can be extremely difficult because the spontaneity is no longer there, but as the improvisation began again, I found that working with an animal gave me another source and another vector to keep me alive. I felt free from my usual judgements and calculations and encountered a series of impulses including a deep desire to make Jackie jump out of the way. For 'wolf' this was a great game! Searching for ways to attack and take Jackie by surprise helped me to be continually present.

## Improvising Using a Shared Image

Cynkutis interrupted our scene work and gathered us in a clear space on the stage to focus us on a new image: 'Remember the tree that you created as a group exercise before? Diane, please find again the vectors and the movement of your tree. After a certain time, others will join you and become different parts of this same tree. Then let this tree find its voice.'

Holding the image of the tree in my mind, I took its vectors into my body, digging my feet into the floor, trying to extend them like roots to ground me. One by one, others came to join me. As we moved, sounds and words emerged. It felt as though our tree was one living being. Cynkutis coached us from the side:

> Do not break your concentration, but with this image that you are part of the same tree, create again your scene for the dividing of the money. You do not need to repeat exactly what you did earlier today, but the impulses are the same. At the same time, do not forget this image of the tree: you are the trunk, the branches, maybe even the leaves of the same tree.

We repeated our improvisation of the family fighting over money but with a stronger sense of kinship. I felt that I was the solid trunk fiercely owning the money and being forced by the others to divide its very lifeblood.

After some time, Cynkutis brought the improvisation to a close: 'We will break now. Tonight, when we meet, you will present your monologue. See you at five.'

### Journal entry, morning of 24 June 1984

*Today's improvisation helped me see how animal associations can give a scene a clear purpose and strong impulses. It seems that whenever I follow Zbyszek's directions clearly and with absolute commitment, my work opens up and I surprise myself. Still, even though I feel good about today, I have no idea how to use these discoveries when I present my monologue tonight.*

CHAPTER NINETEEN

# SYNTHESIS

## Sunday, 24 June 1984: Evening Session in the Theatre

> *In the most important moment, when we really have to work, we must forget everything that we have learned and take this risk.*

When I arrived at the theatre, Cynkutis was alone, leaning against the backstage door looking out at the twilight. He acknowledged my presence, then turned back to drink in this moment in nature, his voice hushed by the sight:

> Beautiful, isn't it? For several days I am looking through this door that opens from the back of the stage into nature, because as evening comes, there is always a time of special light on the trees; it is unbelievable, the play of shadow. Soon will come the moment, and I watch for it. At that time, the presence of this stage—black walls, reflection of light on the wooden beams and, through that door, open air, nature, and the game of light and shadow—reminds me of something that I cannot name. This picture is very meaningful, and I cannot find the meaning. Tomorrow I will take my camera to try to capture it; maybe it will help me to see better. For me this image is deeply connected with my idea of theatre. One day, I will make such a theatre that has this opening into nature.

Soon the others arrived, charged with anticipation for their upcoming presentations. It was helpful that Cynkutis began the evening with strong, physical warm-ups:

> Begin to walk around the space but interrupt your walking with changes in direction. Have a rhythm of determination in your movements. When you hear 'Freeze!' stop immediately in whatever position you are in. Sense the shape that your body makes. What image comes to you from that position? Take a few moments to deepen and expand that picture, then continue walking.

Cynkutis kept us moving at a good pace and did not let us sink into thoughts of what was to come. 'Move with determination!' he called out.

## Body Work with Partners: Exploring a Shared Image

Cynkutis gathered us together:

> In this next task, your body and the body of your partner must keep a point of contact the entire time, but do not use your hands to touch. Your contact must be continuous, but it will also develop and change, moving from touching with one part of the body to another. Do not jump from place to place thinking about what you will do next, the movement is a continuous flow. Let the body suggest what you will do. Use this contact with your partner and the position of your bodies to explore the images I suggest.

Cynkutis began by demonstrating with Jackie, naming 'flying' as their image. As the improvisation developed, their bodies wove and arched over one another, illuminating and revealing this archetypal action in various ways. As usual, Jackie's physical work was precise and clear. Cynkutis was completely engaged. His body rounded and contorted effortlessly to stay true to the shifting point of contact with his partner. Sometimes it was the shoulders, sometimes the calf or the chest, but one part of the body was always touching the other partner. They supported each other's flight, rolling over and around each other as their exploration opened to include falling, suspension, hovering, ecstasy—a variety of possibilities inspired by the configurations and their focus on the image. They were like two fluid statues.

Next, Cynkutis paired the rest of us with a partner. He asked us all to begin our work with the image of 'flight', subsequently changing the image to 'mother and child', 'volcano', and so on. After all these days of work together, the close presence of a partner gave us strength for the task at hand.

## Synthesis: Presentation of Monologues

After a brief break, Cynkutis oriented us to the work ahead:

> Tonight, when you present your monologues, the tools we have investigated will be your partners. You will have the partner of this space and whatever furniture or props you select as well as these lighting instruments and the opposing vectors of light and dark. Before you begin though, I would like you to take time outside to explore again an association from nature for your character. Find the body and voice as well as its vectors.

We went out the open door at the back of the theatre and down the steps. Instead of being worried about our final presentation, we were now focused on one important element—an association for our character. The twilight made everything feel liminal and mysterious.

A large moth fluttered past me. Its movements were quick and erratic. It beat its wings, intending to go in one direction but the vagaries of the wind cast it high and low as though on invisible currents. I felt a stillness come over me . . . why not take this moth as my association for Mary? I had been drawn to the salamander earlier, but that association had kept me on one track: my experience of fear. Why not try this beautiful, hapless creature?

I started taking on elements of its body. Its centre seemed to be the upper chest in the area of the sternum. Starting an impulse from that centre, my arms flew open and rapidly closed, then opened again like wings. I felt a quickening radiating from my chest area through my body that carried with it a shiver of energy. The image of the moth and the resulting movements affected me immediately.

As I continued to work with my chest centre, a bright energy coursed through me. I felt lifted and impelled to rush and sail across the grass. I followed that impulse, doing a few practice 'flights'. I wanted to see if I could continue to be energized and impelled whenever I pulsed these movements outwards from the chest area. Yes, they spoke to my body every time, triggering something energetic that brought me to instant action. I then began to physicalize not just the movement of the wings but the rest of the insect's body as well. As I worked with my face and mouth, I uncovered something hideous: despite the beauty of wings and flight, my face was becoming hardened and distorted as it took on the proboscis, which could only suck nectar, and my hands turned into withered, clutching claws. I felt instinctively that these opposite vectors of beauty and horror could hold some of the secrets of Mary's character. Suddenly there was a sound from above, Cynkutis was standing at the top of the stairs, beckoning us to come in.

While we were gone, he had transformed the space. The auditorium was now completely dark except for two pools of light on the stage. One spot cast a sharp circle of light from stage left onto the centre front, while a more diffuse light covered the middle section. Various boxes, chairs, and props were placed to the side, available if needed.

'Before you begin, I would like to ask something of all of you,' he said speaking slowly and purposefully.

> Please do not focus on trying to remember what we have done in the exercises from before. If it is important, it will come to you in the work, during the work.
>
> In the beginning of our training, we learn as much as possible and try as many things as possible, but in the most important moment, when we really have to work, we must forget everything that we have learned and take this risk. It is like entering paradise

> naked. And it is right to proceed in this way because we will find that everything that we learned will come back in our work. It will not be in exactly the same form as we learned it, but that is why it will be alive.

Judith seemed confused. 'You say that we should forget everything, but aren't we conscious of what the process is when it's happening?' Cynkutis replied:

> Oh yes, it is always very conscious what the actor is doing. Sometimes it is escaping from consciousness if, when the process starts, you are taken into a really big risk. What I was asking was not about consciousness of the process; quite simply I am asking you not to focus on past moments you may have achieved. Focus on your tools, on the partners of the space, lights, and text.
>
> Who would like to begin?

I raised my hand, not wanting to dissipate the energy I had gathered outdoors.

'Arrange the space for your work, please, however you wish. From the place of this association that you have chosen, create your environment.' Cynkutis' voice was strong and clear. His vital presence made me feel that anything was possible.

I stepped onto the stage and began to orient myself. The deep darkness around the two pools of lights felt foreboding. I gazed upwards, letting the strength and position of each lighting instrument slowly sink in. The spotlight was blinding when I looked directly at it, forcing me to look away. The soft glow from the centre light encompassed not only the space on the floor but the air around it, suggesting an arena of light where something could happen.

I dragged a large, rectangular wooden box to the centre of the space and stood it upright like an altar or a pedestal for a work of art that did not exist. I placed a smaller square box in a corner, closer to the audience area. I was not consciously planning how to arrange the elements but was holding on to my recent work outdoors and working intuitively, simply sensing if what I did felt right or not. In the end, I created a partially closed and caged space around the upright box, pooled in a soft light.

Once again, I took in each set piece, sensing them in my body. I observed the different lights, allowing their presences to sink in. They would be my partners in the work.

I walked into the darkness at the back of the stage to prepare. Centring myself, I conjured the image of the moth, tightening my shoulder blades as I imagined its energetic life in my chest. I started to tremble. I felt a shimmering energy moving from my shoulder blades and down my arms. The impulse to move radiated from my sternum and became the pulsing opening and closing of my arms, my wings. As I continued to source the image of the moth, opening and closing my arms more rapidly, I could feel my chest area becoming more and more stimulated. Suddenly, a shimmering beam of what seemed like light entered me from high above, coursing down through my head and into my body. It animated me, and I found myself running and in 'flight' towards the centre of the workspace I had created. The energy that had entered me, this source that I experienced as light, was now directing my improvisation, and I was journeying with it. But even though possessed by the energy, I remained conscious of everything that was occurring.

The partners of set elements and lighting instruments were critical as the two vectors of my moth character came to life and the dramatic underbelly of Mary's monologue played itself out.[1] As I spoke Mary's

---

1 The fuller passage of Mary Tyrone's monologue in Eugene O'Neill's *Long Day's Journey into Night* reads:

> MARY TYRONE: Poor hands! You'd never believe it, but they were once one of my good points, along with my hair and eyes, and I had a fine figure, too.
>
> *Her tone has become more and more far-off and dreamy.*
>
> They were a musician's hands. I used to love the piano. I worked so hard

lines, 'I have two dreams. To be a nun, that was the more beautiful one.' I was a beautiful moth on display. But this angelic, unrealistic dream of beauty was countered by the grotesque reality of what had happened to my hands. Mary's crippled hands were now incarnated in the stick-like legs and grasping claws of an insect, horrible reminders that she was not an angel but some freak of nature. I held them out, knotted and trembling in front of me, as I choked out the lines, 'See, Cathleen, how ugly

---

> at my music in the Convent—if you can call it work when you do something you love. Mother Elizabeth and my music teacher both said I had more talent than any student they remembered. My father paid for special lessons. He spoiled me. He would do anything I asked. He would have sent me to Europe to study after I graduated from the Convent. I might have gone—if I hadn't fallen in love with Mr. Tyrone. Or I might have become a nun. I had two dreams. To be a nun, that was the more beautiful one. To become a concert pianist, that was the other.
>
> *She pauses, regarding her hands fixedly. Cathleen blinks her eyes to fight off drowsiness and a tipsy feeling.*
>
> I haven't touched a piano in so many years. I couldn't play with such crippled fingers, even if I wanted to. For a time after my marriage I tried to keep up my music. But it was hopeless. One-night stands, cheap hotels, dirty trains, leaving children, never having a home—
>
> *She stares at her hands with fascinated disgust.*
>
> See, Cathleen, how ugly they are! So maimed and crippled! You would think they'd been through some horrible accident!
>
> *She gives a strange little laugh.*
>
> So they have, come to think of it.
>
> *She suddenly thrusts her hands behind her back.*
>
> I won't look at them. They're worse than the foghorn for reminding me—
>
> *Then with defiant self-assurance.*
>
> But even they can't touch me now.
>
> *She brings her hands from behind her back and deliberately stares at them—calmly.*
>
> They're far away. I see them, but the pain is gone. (O'Neill: 103–4).

they are! So maimed and crippled! You would think they'd been through some horrible accident!'

I knelt before the pedestal box and prayed, 'I won't look at them.' Then, I swiftly stood up, slamming my clenched fists down on the box as though to break them into pieces. 'They're worse than the foghorn for reminding me.' Everything I had intuitively set up in the space was like a web keeping me linked to the improvisation. As I raised my hands to slam them down again, my eyes were drawn to the spotlight above. Whereas before I could not even look at it full, now I was transfixed. My hands fell to my side, limp and forgotten. The light was intoxicating beauty, it was the drug I could not live without, the narcotic that would lead to death, just as fire consumes the moth. 'But even they can't touch me now. They're far away. I see them, but the pain is gone.' As I spoke the text, I drank in the light, hypnotized and absorbed completely by it.

When the improvisation came to an end, I was weak from the effort and stunned by what I had experienced. At every point in the improvisation, I'd been led by some kind of force beyond my control.

As I took my seat with the others, Cynkutis asked, 'What was your association?'

'A moth.'

For a few moments he was silent and then responded, 'Very precise.'

Jackie was the next to begin her monologue, but I was so preoccupied I could hardly pay attention. Something other than myself had led me in the work, though I had still been fully conscious. Was this the 'trance' that was referred to in the work of the Laboratory Theatre? The only other monologue that day that seemed to come from the same mysterious place was David's.

David's work focused on the sharp pool of light at the front of the stage. The only other element he partnered with was his shirt. Working with the character of Jamie, the troubled, conflicted son, David began his monologue in the darkness, just outside the circle of light, tugging at his shirt in the chest area near the heart as though something was troubling him there, buried deep within him yet still active and rising like a blister.

Slowly, he made his way towards the light, hesitantly entering it, as though, as the light touched him, it could reveal his naked self underneath. His half-lit face was attracted by the spotlight yet could not endure its full force. Holding on to his shirt/heart, he pulled back into the shadows. In a darkened voice, he spoke words from his monologue until he was drawn towards the light once more. When his face was again half-lit, he tugged and wrestled quietly with his shirt, pulling it away from his heart as he retreated into the darkness again. Comfortable with neither darkness nor light, David showed someone in extreme existential conflict. His work was simple yet profound and seemed guided by some inner force emanating from the chest area. Each impulse that he had was totally organic. You could clearly see that he was drinking from a source.[2]

---

2 David commented on his association for the monologue and his experience that night:

> A vulture or buzzard was the animal I was operating through. Embodying that—the energy of a buzzard circling and circling over this carrion. Jamie was an alcoholic and kind of a nihilist. A vulture really seemed to suit that monologue. I'm flying above the decay looking for an opportunity for nourishment, looking for an opportunity to pick at the decay of the family, but flying above it. Not really willing to be part of it. I was also feeling a sort of despair. It felt like despair and detachment all at the same time. Those are the feelings I remember.
>
> I do remember picking at my shirt. I'm not sure if it was conscious. We were learning all kinds of techniques. I remember Zbyszek saying that the way that you interact with objects, the way you touch an object, can bring you into a state. It can help you enter a particular state. I was not a vibrant and healthy vulture. I was older or sick, you know, maybe when I touched the shirt, I was picking at feathers that were coming out. It was sort of conscious and also not conscious. That night, it was like some sort of channelling experience. It really was remarkable. I mean, it was a remarkable thing to experience it myself. So, I'm not even really going to take any credit for it. (Saperstein, personal communication, February 2024)

Cynkutis was quieter than I expected at the end of our monologues. He simply thanked us for the day's work, saying we would start a new investigation tomorrow. The day of presentations over, we headed back to our dorm rooms, absorbed in thought.

### Journal Entry, evening of 24 June 1984

*Why isn't Zbyszek astonished when all these crazy things are happening in the work? It must mean he knows a lot about these processes. He said my association of the moth was 'very precise'. The Moth!! That association opened up not only the monologue but a field of energy carrying me along. This must be how associations work when they are right. Still, if I hadn't taken in the lights or the set pieces and their particular presences as my partners, the work wouldn't have opened up.*

CHAPTER TWENTY

# KEEP YOUR SEARCH ALIVE

## Monday, 25 June 1984: Daytime Session at the Theatre and Library

> *The idea is to face again new circumstances, new possibilities, to be open to everything that is in front of us. That is an artistic attitude.*

When we gathered at the theatre, Cynkutis informed us that our morning session would involve individual research at the Hamilton College library. He prepared us by speaking once again of the importance of keeping our curiosity alive, always reaching for what is unknown. He made it clear that without this attitude, the work does not have the same possibilities.[1]

### Conversation: Keep Your Search Alive

> For acting, or for any art, it is absolutely important to drink from a lot of things. Otherwise, how can we associate? Associations are the result of a permanently alive brain which is connecting and clicking together things.
>
> Art doesn't happen without curiosity. Art happens when people with courage are trying to invent and to develop new skills and new possibilities. Improvising on the basis of knowledge.

1 For an in-depth discussion of the process-oriented way the Laboratory Theatre approached training, see Chapter Six in Kumiega (1985: 109–26).

Using the knowledge of what has gone before, not to conserve achievements, but to create a new path.

One of the most beautiful examples of how important it is to improvise on the basis of knowledge—never without knowledge—is Columbus. He knew a lot about navigation, geography, circumstances on the ocean, psychology, and how to lead people, and he was a very brave man. When he applied to the King of Spain for a boat to discover a shorter trip to India, by sailing west instead of east, he did it because he got information that there are these crazy guys who are thinking that the earth is round—but no one before confirmed it. It was an act of incredible courage for someone to take this idea seriously and to make a trip. There was an incredible investment of risk, and *by the way* he discovered America, *by the way*.

This is a beautiful example of what it means when someone is working. Someone is preparing their body, someone is preparing their voice, someone is learning a lot about the abilities of human nature, including psychology, including reading literature, including looking at paintings, including collecting as much information as possible, always being ready to take in something like a new idea. And when this new idea, not even confirmed by someone else before, calls to your spirit and is saying, 'Take me, take this risk,' you are taking a risk. Because you can take this risk if you are doing something for yourself permanently—like training for the body, training for the voice, and learning.

I think it is a very important attitude for artists: this desire to gain knowledge and learning. And do not confirm what you know already! Because what you know already is not everything that you need. Everything that we know is interesting as long as we don't know it, while we are receiving it. In the moment in which we know it, it is no longer interesting. If it works for us, we have to use it for keeping ourselves in good shape, for training.

But the idea is to face again new circumstances, new possibilities, to be open to everything that is in front of us. That is an artistic attitude.

## Sourcing Paintings and Their Vectors (I)

Cynkutis said:

Today we will look for sources for our work in art—in paintings. Something that can inform our feelings.

**[Audio #15]** Feeling must come to us. We are obliged to find the road to feeling using our voice and body, the theatrical environment, everything that we know about acting. Feeling is like the crown which makes that everything that we develop is getting heart, it is getting pulse, it is getting spirit.

During the time of preparation, when you are reading the play, when you do analyse what is in this material sometimes you name a feeling. Like for instance: in this character is a lot of joy. If, with this idea, you will go to a Museum of Art or take albums and search through pictures of different painters trying to find something which is of joyful times, you can find such a picture. You are starting an investigation: Why am I receiving an expression of joy in this picture? What makes this expression actively? And you are developing parts of your body, parts of your construction which somehow can be used by you if you want to express joy. Still it is just like touching something in your body. You are not going to use it literally on the stage. You study. You are collecting material about the play you are going to make.

During the time of rehearsing when you will improvise something from the movement you did in front of the picture [the feeling of joy] can return and if it will return it will be for you like a confirmation that something you are doing is touching a very obvious expression from your body. Something is going on. That's why it is very important to be close to everything in art that is done and to be familiar with it. Because there is not only something that stimulates our research but there is also confirmation of the sources from which art is coming. The art of the actor is coming from the same source as the art of the painter or art of the sculptor. You are doing it through your body.

It is not only theological, it is practical if you, watching the sculpture of Michelangelo's *Pietà,* try to find what are the vectors in this sculpture—how she [Mother Mary] is giving this body and how this body is built in her arms. You are touching, definitely, something that is very sensual and is very inspiring. But it is not because you have such an idea in your mind but because you are preparing yourself to play a theatrical piece in which there is a relationship between mother and son.

For instance, Mary [Tyrone], whatever we think about her, she is a mother and it will be interesting to find out why she really doesn't connect with her sons. She already feels the death of Edmund before he dies. She's a terrible mother. She is only complaining and full of fear but she is doing nothing to protect him against death. She is not fighting with Tyrone to send him to the best physicians and to the best places. She is escaping from confrontation with death. It is another dimension of Mary.

If you will take, for instance, not how wrong she is but if you will start an investigation of what is an expression of motherhood—for instance, the *Pietà* is such a symbol—the actress playing the mother, Mary [Tyrone], with the actor playing Edmund can make such an investigation [taking on the sculptural form of the *Pietà*]. And later, they talk. And later, they talk. And it really never can happen for Mary [this expression of love]. Because Mary will try to avoid touching your sick body. How important that information is! How important that information is means, practically, that the actress playing Mary is always coming close

> to Eddy but touch is something that she wants to avoid. Touch is something that scares her. She is touching and escaping to the window. Do you understand? This gives you information? Do you understand how we came to this possibility? Just to intellectualize, you cannot get it.

'But do you intellectualize too much if you say Mary is sometimes like a little child?' Jackie asked.

'Oh no!' Cynkutis responded.

'Mary is in a drug haze. Mary is in a dream! Can you look for a painting like that?' Leanne chimed in.

'Exactly,' Cynkutis replied with approval.

'You know what else would not be intellectualizing?' Judith said. 'Mary was at a special kind of convent school. So all those nun pictures and convent pictures had such a profound effect on that girl.'

Encouraged by the contributions of the group, Cynkutis enlarged the discussion:

> So, you know what you are building? You are building the biography of your character because what your eye really sees is, in a good sense, a substitute for a biography. Like whatever we know from our past tense, whatever happened to us, made our biography. But it really was something that happened: what we touched by our eye, by our hands, by our body. We did smell it. When you are watching the picture and working with this picture it is like to build this biography. There is something later in your memory you can connect in your thoughts: 'She as a nun.' If you selected from the painting certain shape of 'nun', when she is talking about herself as a nun, you see this picture in this moment. And this picture which was actively investigated by you creates in your body a certain *response* when she is talking about herself as a nun: 'I was in a convent'. And the body remembers how it was in this convent. But it comes from the picture, you know, it is something that is leading you. You understand what I mean?

'Yeah,' Leanne replied. 'It just seems there are so many possibilities for each character that we can be looking for. Like the animals . . . '

'Definitely. Definitely,' Cynkutis continued to elaborate:

> There are thousands of possibilities but you are not only going to the library to search for pictures you are doing something with this picture. Because you know something about vectors. You are not only going to the zoo to watch this animal. You know something about vectors. You are trying to understand what made this animal so expressive. Why you feel connection between this animal and the part you are going to play. Stanislavski talked about biography. An actor has to create a biography for the part he is playing, for the role. It [source work with animals and paintings] is a possibility to create such a biography. **[End Audio #15]**
>
> With this in mind, to prepare for our work this evening, I want you to make an investigation at the library. Search for and study paintings that somehow speak to you of your character and of elements in your scene. Find the vectors that create this picture and practice taking them into your body. Do not forget the objects in the picture! Look for what joins and what separates the elements. Drink from these pictures as much as you can. We will use your explorations when we work together this evening.

We spent the rest of the morning at the campus library, looking through art books, searching for what spoke to us in the colours, objects, and in the body positions of the people depicted. When we found a painting that we felt would associate, we carefully looked for opposing vectors, light versus dark as well as the shapes and angles that created tension and movement.

I gazed a long time at Rembrandt's *Descent from the Cross*. After my monologue last night in which vectors of light and dark appeared so strongly, I was drawn to his careful use of those elements. He made manifest the spirituality of light.

As I took the lines and angles of the figures in the painting into my body, it became clear to me that Rembrandt had utilized vectors, the tension of opposing forces. 'Don't forget the objects in the picture,' Cynkutis had said, 'Look for what joins and what separates the elements.' The whole picture became dynamically alive as I followed the vectors, adjusting my body as I gazed.

I was also fascinated by a portrait of Saint Catherine as a young girl. Her sweet smile and slightly bent head reminded me of Mary Tyrone's image of herself when she was young. Could I use this portrait as Mary's memory of herself when she was a young girl dreaming of the convent? From previous discussions, it seemed that Cynkutis wanted us to look for what animated and moved *us*, not what we thought would move an imaginary character. This picture spoke so strongly to me that I decided to use it as a source.

On my way back from the library, I stopped to gaze at the dramatic poster of *Apocalypsis Cum Figuris* displayed in the theatre office's window. It was almost four feet high, a print made from the original woodcut depicting a mythic scene: the moment that the biblical chapter of 'Revelations' was revealed. I was completely absorbed in looking at it when I suddenly realized Cynkutis was nearby, silently observing me as I examined the poster. '*Apocalypsis*,' he said with amusement walking over to join me, 'our last piece created for the theatre.' We stood looking at the poster and, for a fleeting moment, he seemed quiet with remembrances from the past, but then, decisively, he broke the spell:

> You know I am returning to Poland and, in the Laboratory space, I will begin again with the creation of another company, a second vector: 'Second Studio'. There will also be an international company. Why don't you come and join the work? It will take time for things to be ready but, if you want, make arrangements to come.

'If I want?! Of course, I do!' I thought. But all I said was, 'Yes, I would like that.' I walked back to the dorm on a cloud. It was a dream come true!

CHAPTER TWENTY-ONE

# RHYTHM

## Monday, 25 June 1984: Evening Session in the Theatre

> *Often you hear me say: 'Acting is a source of energy.' [ . . . ] The actor is a generator. He is able to produce, evoke energy.*

The twilight was quite beautiful and, as we gathered, it brought with it a softness. We were all aware this would be one of our last working sessions together.

### Sourcing Paintings and Their Vectors (II)

Cynkutis greeted us individually before beginning the work: 'Today, using vectors, I want you to bring the two of the paintings you found into your bodies. Work with one painting then the other one. Do not make this an imitation from the outside; find the opposing forces in your bodies to create the dynamic tension, the *life*, of each of your paintings.'

We explored the task for quite a while and then, one by one, we presented our work to him. After he had observed where we were in the process, he enlarged upon the task: 'Take on the vectors of one of your paintings and then move slowly into the vectors that create the second painting. In the transition between these two paintings find the place in yourself that is "in-between". This is a place of possibility and a different kind of life. Speak a line of your text from that precise place.'

We did as he instructed, trying to find this place within ourselves, the place 'in-between'. As I moved between the strong vectors of Rembrandt's *Descent from the Cross* and the softer edged portrait of Saint

Catherine—all the while trying to stay in the place in-between—I had an unusual experience of myself and the text. It was a poetic image: as though a loving face was hovering over the crucible of the cross and 'touching' that experience with her words.

As we were taking time, writing in our journals, Cynkutis came over to me. He said he'd been thinking about the energy that sometimes overwhelmed me in my work, referring to my character work with the salamander and my memory work with fear. He said he had an exercise with rhythm in mind to address it. 'Come onto the stage,' he said to everyone, 'it can be good for all, this work with rhythm.'

## Sourcing Rhythm

Cynkutis pulled large wooden boxes into a loose circle. He sat on one and drummed a rhythm as we gathered: 'Everything has a rhythm. For this last exercise we will use rhythm as our source.'

I remembered hearing that each member of the Laboratory Theatre was responsible for the development of different aspects of training. Cynkutis had developed the work with rhythm.[1]

'Diane, we will begin. If someone can please suggest to us a theme?'

'Love,' said Elizabeth.

'So, Diane, with this theme to explore, choose something from nature that you can associate with love.' He stood by the boxes where he had just pounded out a rhythm awaiting my reply.

I focused on my experiences of romantic love, searching for an association for that clinging magnetic energy. 'It reminds me of ivy, of a climbing vine,' I ventured.

---

1 'Each day [ . . . ] the actors did exercises organized by members of the troupe. Mirecka was instructor for plasticity of gesture and movement. Molik taught breathing and vocal exercises. Cynkutis taught rhythm exercises, and Ryszard Cieślak taught acrobatics and mastery of the body. In addition to this, Grotowski conducted so-called "etudes" or vocal composition exercises' (Osiński 1986: 70).

Cynkutis seemed surprised:

> Really? For me it is fire. Well, we will see that it does not even have to be the same association that we have. We also do not need to know what association our partner is using in the work which can often be better.
>
> Find the rhythm for your association and for this theme of love. Rhythm brings a specific energy and can lead you in a certain direction. Keep the rhythm and absorb it into your body; keep it somewhere in your body, using it as a source to drink from in the improvisation. If you feel that you have lost contact with the rhythm, you can return to it strongly, making it with your feet or on the boxes once more.

Focusing on my association, I beat out a rhythm on one of the boxes with my hands. As I pounded it out, envisioning the ivy plant's growth, I felt a tightening in the area above the solar plexus. My arms felt heavy and full of an energy seeking release. But these sensations did not last, so I strengthened the rhythm to summon the image back again. Each time I tried to use rhythm to conjure the image, it evoked an energetic wave that rose up in me only to quickly dissipate like water through a sieve.

Cynkutis had begun his rhythm at the boxes and then moved out into the open space. He was in vibrant motion and I decided to join him. I intensified my own rhythm, not just through my hands but through my feet as well. As I moved away from the boxes, pounding out the rhythm with each step, I began to recite some of my text—my voice slipping into its usual tense, high-pitched tone.

'Less voice, less emotion,' called out Cynkutis. His voice had a rich, distinctive quality, shaped by the rhythm and imagery that was unfolding within him.

I tried to cut back on the emotion in my voice, but when I did so, everything I had developed seemed to drain out of me. Back to the boxes

I went to source the rhythm. But when I started to recite my text, my voice again became pinched and my body clenched up.

'Try with only the body,' Cynkutis urged.

My feet stomped, my arms twined, and my body twirled. Cynkutis came closer to me and then moved towards the edges of the space shaking his hands out to demonstrate how to shake excess energy off by using the hands and the whole body. I followed him, attempting to do the same.

The beginnings of an improvisation began, consisting of our coming closer then moving apart, but my commitment to the image of the ivy and my ability to use this rhythmic source waxed and waned. 'Keep the rhythm,' he said, 'It must be kept. It builds and it energizes.'

I was having difficulty staying with my image, so I returned to the boxes to begin again. Cynkutis was moving quickly around the space and, as I bent low over the boxes and reconnected with the energy of the vine, he scooped me up in his arms and lifted me over his head, spinning my curled body aloft. As he began to put me down, my feet reached for the floor, my whole body stretching like the strong tendril of an extending vine. The improvisation evolved. I had the drooping, clinging quality of the vine while he had the strong engagement of fire, moving swiftly around me or raising me aloft. Then, slowing his rhythm, he began to lead me back to the boxes. Our whole focus was now on our hands as they beat out a contained rhythm on the boxes, slowing the tempo, bringing the energy down until, at last, there was silence. The improvisation was at an end.

Cynkutis was breathing hard from the exertion, but he did not rest.

'Judith come,' he said. 'Theme, please?'

'Spring,' she said.

'Association?'

'A seed beginning to sprout,' she answered.

'So, we shall both work with the same image.'

From the very beginning, Judith matched Cynkutis with a forceful rhythm on the boxes. It pounded out strong and primordial, building in intensity until the energy of it moved them out into the space. Their whole bodies were now contracting and expanding to the pulse. They came closer together and clasped hands with Cynkutis' right hand holding Judith's left throughout the rest of the improvisation. Like a mirror image, they bent in towards each other, hands still held, their outer arms pulsing down again and again towards the ground between them, building energy until their bodies opened exuberantly out, their free arms flying out and open to the sky. They repeated this dance, down to the ground between them and then out, over and over again. The vital energy of the image Judith had chosen was manifested in this life affirming dance. It was spring, and the seeds were sprouting, joyful, and alive.

Cynkutis did not rest. Elizabeth, David, and Jackie all had a turn improvising with him. It was a beautiful last session of work together.

CHAPTER TWENTY-TWO

# A FINAL GATHERING

## Tuesday, 26 June 1984: Outdoors at Cynkutis' Residence

*If I am opening your minds and stimulating you to think and to search, that is definitely what I want to do. It is the best thing that can happen in this workshop.*

### Conversation: Making This Process Your Own

After a morning spent packing our belongings, we joined Zbyszek, Jola, and their seven-year-old daughter, Anna, at a picnic table outside their home to share a last meal together. Jola had made traditional Polish dishes including homemade pierogi and a delicious diced-potato salad that had pickles, eggs, ham, and what seemed like a dozen more ingredients. The sun was bright, the mood was merry, and there was a cool breeze blowing. But when the meal was finished, quiet settled in. We were preoccupied with our departure and thinking how empty it would feel when we no longer had this vital presence to challenge and guide us.

David was the first to speak:

**[Audio #16]** Something I was wondering . . . all we can talk about is this work and what we're going to do when we leave. Because we've dangled our feet in this water, Diane and I were talking about this today, but we haven't gone swimming yet. We're just getting a taste of this. And we've got to keep going from here!

Cynkutis replied:

David, this question is already a pragmatic question—still it is good. And it will be a very good question if you will add to your question the next part: 'I put my legs into this water, I don't know how to swim, but it *is important* that I know that there *is* such water into which I can put my feet. And, if it is something valuable for me, maybe not rapidly, but in certain moments of my experiences it will let me go deeper into the water.'

Believe me, those things which we are touching during this workshop, they will return to you in many different circumstances. And if they will return, you will assimilate them, and no longer will they be mine; they will be yours. You will invent them from a new point of view, and you will swallow them. I can only put seeds from which it will grow. When it will grow, there will not be my presence. Everything will be yours, and it must be like that. If you will find, in your schools, in your practice, that it does provide you with certain attitudes and knowledge and it works for you, I am absolutely sure, like it was the last fifteen years, we will meet again. Because everyone who worked with me and for whom my workshop initiates something in thinking and investigation, I don't know how it works, but those people are meeting with me permanently, not for workshops, but for practice. They are bringing their conclusions which they want to confirm or to confront.

My life is devoted for theatre. I am going back to Poland, not to spend my life in Poland, but to run an institute which will spray seeds among other people and will provide those ones who want to come [a chance] to invest more. But, at the same time, if you will find something that is working for you and if you will start to use it more, if you will start to share with someone with whom you are working, you can find that you don't need *me*. Because you can find a different way, your very own way, which is the most valuable.

It is very important what I am talking about now. Do not be afraid that something can disappear. Everything that is valuable never disappears. It is only returning somehow through different experiences.

I took such a workshop with a master of Noh theatre. I learned a lot, believe me, and I had the feeling that I am not going to use this knowledge. So I felt OK because I learned something, but . . . useless! Useless! And one day we talked, and I said, 'Master, I feel very painful because I learned a lot. I feel that my luggage is much more heavy and I am taking something with me . . . ' He finished my sentence: ' . . . and you will never use it.' I said, 'That's exactly what I feel.'

He watched me, and he said, 'But don't throw it away. You are returning to your work. As long as you know your work from the past tense, you cannot think how you can use it. But the work which you are doing has also a future tense. Do you really know what you will do with it?'

I said, 'No, I barely know what I will do with it. I only know what I did.' He said, 'So, keep your luggage with you. Keep it. Maybe in the future you will find something.'

Five years later, I started to use things from him. Five years later it returned and, for instance, those things which I am using with you with voice are stimulated by him—a lot of things are stimulated by him—like voice. Only I was not able to go totally through his understanding because his cultural difference made a certain limit for my understanding. So you don't see; because it is like a wall.

When I was older and I didn't feel any more this difference of the culture, but I stayed in front of a real problem, it returned to me what he was talking about.

Four years ago, I met with him. It was funny because he did remember my question and he said, 'So, man, let's yawn!' He started yawning, and I yawned. So we yawned for five minutes. Sitting in one place, yawning, and he said, 'Oh, I see you learned something from me. You are taking something. You are using something from what we did.' And I smiled, because it was

> exactly by yawning that I developed what he meant. Yawning was the element which helped me to return to the knowledge he passed to me by voice. By yawning. **[End Audio #16]**

Cynkutis looked around at our small group of five, taking each of us in. The moment felt both intimate and profound as he addressed us with kindness and clarity:

> You are very young. If you will seriously select theatre, in front of you is not only the goal of your artistic career, but in front of you is an incredible duty: how much can you stimulate people with whom you will work, people among whom you will be for research, how can you treat theatre as an important element for humankind? Not only providing audiences with entertainment. If theatre is only entertainment, it must be a very empty theatre. Theatre which is looking for entertainment is like a computer trying to guess what six hundred people like.
>
> Opposite to this question is another question: How can people be touched? What can touch them? What can stimulate them? What do they want or what don't they want to see? What are they trying to exclude from their lives? What are they missing? What is missed in our life because of the economy or politics or because of the form of social life? Or what are our dreams? And from answering these questions you can find, in a Shakespeare play, in a Molière play, in other plays, a lot of reasons why you want to do it. So it is not showing on the stage a play, but *selecting* a play through which you want to touch something that is missed, or you want to stimulate thoughts which are disappearing. You can fight for values! You can fight for principles! You can break principles! You can break values! Theatre is an incredible possibility. It is like from the other side of the revolution. Without the revolution penetrating you never saw it. Is it clear what I am trying to say?

'Yes,' we responded with one voice.

So, in this sense, if I am opening your minds and stimulating you to think and to search . . . Oh, definitely I want to do it! And I think it is the biggest thing that can happen. And if truth or knowledge, practical knowledge how to search for something new, helps you with your development, it will be great . . . it will be great.

Everything that I know is the result of my meetings with others who, as I have tried with you, they did for me. They were opening my mind and shaping my consciousness and, very often, showing me how stupid I am and how blind I am. I was spending months or years in total darkness, absolutely doubting everything I knew because they made my world turn upside down. I even blamed them, and I was angry with them. But, after one year or two years, I found that it was very necessary what I went through. I know that we want to select the easiest path through the world, but the easiest path makes us extremely comfortable. I am very thankful still for those who didn't let me select such a narrow way.

What came from them became mine, and whatever you will take from me will be yours in time.

'Thank you for the workshop,' Jackie said.

'Anything else we can put in our suitcases?' joked Judith. Cynkutis tilted his head and smiled. 'I think you will take many things already. And you will see, in your own work and in the work of others, what is there and—which is also important—what is not there.'

He disappeared into his apartment for a few moments and then reappeared brandishing a camera. 'I always take a picture of my students so that I will remember them. So . . . I am going to ask Jola to capture us!' We gathered close together—a completely different group from when we started. Cynkutis, playful as always, arranged not only himself but each of us in the pose he wished: he and David involved in an exchange of glances, Elizabeth looking doubtful, Judith with head bowed regally, Jackie strong and pensive, and I, for some reason, looking straight at the camera as Jola snapped the photo.

FIGURE 13. LEFT TO RIGHT: Zbigniew Cynkutis, Elizabeth Forrester, Jacqueline Kim, David E. Saperstein, Diane Edgecomb, and Judith Archer. *Photograph by Jola Cynkutis. Courtesy of David E. Saperstein.*

---

1 Judith Archer shared her thoughts about Cynkutis' arrangement of us for the photo:

> I think it's incredibly symbolic! First of all, we're all linked together . . . we're all touching each other. Zbyszek is strong, forceful even though his hands are in his pockets. Elizabeth has linked both her hands through his arm—looking for more. Jackie, leaning on David, seems to be puzzled. Unsure if she has 'got it'. David is directly engaged with Zbyszek, leaning towards him. He understands and he is smiling widely! Really happy. David has his arm casually around your neck and you are looking forward. You got it!! You're ready to charge forward with the work . . . the sun is

That simple picture, our memories, journals, and four audiocassettes would be all that physically remained of that time. But inside each of us was a hope that this work that had touched us so deeply would remain.

---

full on your face . . . You and David have your hands on me, touching the nape of my neck, and my head is tilted down, eyes closed. I am overwhelmed with gratitude for what I/we just experienced! My life and my work in theatre, public school and Community Theater was forever changed . . . when that happens what more can you do but bow your head? (Personal communication, 19 February 2024).

## A NOTE IN CLOSING

One month after the workshop, while on a trip to Europe with my sister Martha, I travelled to see Zbyszek and Jola in Wrocław, Poland. As the train pulled into the station, Zbyszek ran beside it, full of youthful enthusiasm. 'Look,' he said as he greeted me, 'the first bird has returned to the ark!' But despite his lightness and energy, everything around looked bleak. Although martial law had been lifted the previous year, the restrictions on daily life imposed by the military junta were very much in effect. The military was everywhere. Troops were marching to martial songs in the parks, soldiers were prevalent on the trolley cars, and the pressure on the people to conform was reflected in stark terms by a local museum's outdoor sculpture exhibit in which an artist had depicted rows of faceless people with all expression erased. Everything seemed to be breaking or broken. Shop windows were empty of goods and food was in short supply. After standing in line for half a day for their ration of meat, Zbyszek spread what little he had on the kitchen table exclaiming, 'This is how I am supposed to feed my family for a month?'

But Cynkutis was clearly not bowed. He was working hard on his plans for a new beginning with his Second Studio of Wrocław. I felt honoured that he and Jola took precious time from their responsibilities to welcome us with both warmth and generosity. When we visited a local theatre to see a play and found it was shuttered, Zbyszek changed plans on the spot, taking us to see the other famous sights of Wrocław: the iconic 'lover's bridge', the central square with its historic painted buildings, and the Laboratory Theatre space where the worn and heavy shoes

FIGURE 14. Zbigniew Cynkutis in rehearsal.
*Photograph by Marek Grotowski. Courtesy of Richard Mennen.*

of *Akropolis* were on display, empty and waiting, in the brick-walled performance space that had seen so much incredible work.

When I declared that my sister and I were off to Brussels next, he declared: 'What a tragedy! Brussels is so bourgeois!' The following day he stood in line for hours for plane tickets that would take us straight to Amsterdam. I remember holding my breath as I watched him dart skilfully, on foot, through dangerous traffic, to commandeer a cab for our next day's pre-dawn ride to the airport, using our unreported US dollars to seal the deal.

Before our leave-taking, we all stayed up late into the night toasting the future of Second Studio with ice-cold shots of Poland's famous bison-weed vodka: Żubrówka. As usual, Cynkutis was provocative and lively, full of irony and dry humour. He questioned us about our lives, bantering with us, though underneath it all I had the feeling his questions were a way of subtly taking our measure. Certainly, my sister impressed him with her gutsy approach to life and her ability to sidestep any direct answer to his questions: 'Martha,' he said to her with real approval in his eyes, 'you are someone I could steal horses with!'

After I returned to the US, Cynkutis and I continued to correspond as I searched for ways both to continue the work we had begun and to make the necessary arrangements to join the work in Poland. In early 1987, I took a workshop with Zygmunt Molik, Cynkutis' close friend and colleague, sponsored by Double Edge Theatre which was in residence at St. Luke's Church in Allston, Massachusetts. It was from Molik that I heard the terrible news that Zbyszek had died in a car accident. Judith, my colleague from the Hamilton College intensive, was there with me. We sat on the front steps of the church where the workshop was being held in stunned disbelief. The impossible had happened and we, like the countless others who were guided by Cynkutis, would have to carry on as best we could.

Through the years, I have kept many things 'in my suitcase', gradually bringing forward the treasures that Cynkutis had given in the light of my own work. Knowing the gift that I had in the extensive audio recordings of the workshop, in 2000 I began transcribing them. When I shared what I was doing with Richard Mennen and told him of my wish to publish these transcripts, he said, 'To really make sense, they're going to need your experience of the workshop alongside them.' Thus began the journey of this book.

Cynkutis' voice, his words, his exercises, his dream of a theatre with an 'opening into nature' are in these pages. The knowledge he had of the depth and beauty of the acting profession can be sourced here. His warnings of the dangers of a life that cannot see beyond 'killing pragmatism' rings even truer today in our woefully concrete and material world. And his devotion to his calling as a theatre artist, a dedication that bordered on ascetism and eschewed an easy path, reminds us of the prize that true commitment to an ideal can achieve: the activation of core spiritual values that can sustain us and provide meaning in our lives.

The processes Cynkutis evoked in us in our intensive have accompanied me every step of my own artistic path from the creation of my solo theatre piece *Restraints*[1] (2010) to my ongoing work as a performance-oriented storyteller embodying both mythic and personal tales. What was, for me, a revelation: the inseparable trinity of Voice–Body–Image is now a part of every workshop I lead. Cynktuis' teachings have helped me to intuit and embody the deep archetypes I find in mythology, to access the primal power of naming and to link my work to nature as a source, enriching not only my performances but my life, while his emphasis on process and discovery *by the way* keeps my craft open to possibility.

---

1 *Restraints*, which premiered at Charlestown Working Theater, Charlestown, MA, was developed over a period of five years with guidance and support from Jola Cynkutis. The work modes used to develop the piece were drawn from the summer workshop with Cynkutis, augmented by Jola's exercises and advice, as well as training and performance processes explored while performing and creating work with Double Edge Theatre in the late 1980s and early 1990s.

I hope that this book will stimulate others and spark renewed interest in the extraordinary accomplishments of the Polish Laboratory Theatre. May it bring remembrance to those who knew Cynkutis and renewal to those who still hear the sound of the calling that first drew them to the theatre arts and to what we called, in those days, with both affection and honour, 'the work'.

## ACKNOWLEDGMENTS

Along the path of this writing, I've experienced many moments of serendipity and received help from many 'companions on the road'. How lonely the way would have been without Cynkutis' dear friend and colleague Richard Mennen at my side. He guided this book from its initial phase onwards with insight, provocation, laughter, and many a late-night story-sharing session with him and his wife Sally.

Jola Cynkutis believed deeply in the importance of this account, related, as it is, from *inside* the process. I'm grateful not only for her support but her uncompromising approach to the work, which never wavered with the passage of years. She gave selflessly of her time, knowledge, talents, and shared with me her home and studio space in Poland. She sustained me with her deep friendship as she filled in gaps in my training and helped me develop a solo piece based on these processes.

Zbyszek's amazing daughters, Anna and Magda, have given me boundless energy and support along with additional reasons to finish this manuscript. Their provocative, insightful eyes and powerful nature reminds me always of the gifts of their father.

This book would not be the same without the strength, grace, and clarity of Jenna Kumiega. Whoever has her at their side is thrice blessed. A brilliant and nuanced writer she befriended this work. Clarifying and reviewing it with the insight that can only come from intimate familiarity with the work and the people involved.

Magda Cynkutis-Simon and Robert Simon brought such life-force to the project. Their input, support, and help carried me through the end of the writing process just when I needed it most.

Paul Allain was essential all through the course of this writing. Like the knights of old, he rescued me from untold conundrums: answering esoteric questions, dissolving obstacles, solving problems. Thank you, Paul.

To so many I am deeply indebted for their thoughts, help and support. Tom Kingdon, professor of film at Emerson College, championed this project with careful editing and insight. I'm indeed fortunate that his search and mine overlapped as I struggled to codify this work. Tom Megan, my clarion-minded husband, brought invaluable insight and questions. Margot Chamberlain, my harper and friend, selflessly pulled me out of the mud as I floundered with the rigours of style. Other blessings include: Maria Cynkutis' unwavering support and generosity of heart; Khalid Tyabji's friendship and help, Dominika Laster's editing skill and deep presence; Penny Post's enthusiasm; Jay O'Callahan's irreplaceable ears; Huck Bennert and Matthew Megan's rescue of Cynkutis' voice from the Terrain of Ancient Audio; Dennis Toohey's photo editing skills; the timely grant from the Regina Mundi Foundation as well as funds from individual donors, and Kickstarter friends which gave the project the financial support it needed; and the important gift from Anna Cynkutis and Khalid Tyabji of the Bill Ireland illustrations, developed by Cynkutis, to grace the pages on physical exercises.

I also call out to those who shared my search for a theatre so powerful it could express the deepest part of our nature. For the amazing times we shared on worn, wooden floors, barefoot and brave in search of the impossible: Judith Archer, Maggie Browning, Nachum Cohen, Bonnie Cordon, Amelia Cox, Robin Doty, Kermit Dunkelberg, Wendy Flagg, Elizabeth Forrester, Michael Balcanoff, David Flaxman, Sarah Hickler, Ellen Kaplan, Jacqueline Kim, Kevin Kuhlke, Kim Mancuso, David Russell, David E. Saperstein, Sheryl Stoodley, M. J. Toohey, and many others. May the search continue albeit in different guise!

A last and very special thanks to David E. Saperstein, whose love for this work caused him to flip on a tape recorder at Cynkutis' 1984 summer workshop at Hamilton College. I cannot thank him enough for this gift he gave to the world. The entire treasure trove of audio he captured, is now digitized and enhanced, and will be available for educational and research purposes at the Grotowski Institute in Wrocław, Poland.

*Source Work for Actors*
AUDIO EXCERPTS

Audio excerpts from Zbigniew Cynkutis' June 1984 workshop at Hamilton College, Clinton, New York, which form the foundation of this book and are quoted throughout, are available on a dedicated YouTube channel created to accompany this volume.

Readers can access the recordings by scanning the adjacent QR code or visiting the url:

https://www.youtube.com/playlist?list=PLmk97Q-BPKXR5LxL97jUlnQKnTb12Bvew

## WORKS CITED

ALLAIN, Paul. 2015. 'Preface', in *Acting with Grotowski: Theatre as a Field for Experiencing Life* (Khalid Tyabji trans.; Paul Allain and Khalid Tyabji eds). London and New York: Routledge, pp. xii–xxiv.

CHRISTOFF, Catharine. 2017. *Rethinking Religion in the Theatre of Grotowski.* Abingdon and New York: Routledge.

CYNKUTIS, Zbigniew. 1982. Complete audio recording of an interview with Robert Findlay. Kansas, 26 May. From the archives of Jola Cynkutis.

CYNKUTIS, Zbigniew. 1984. Sound recordings of Cynkutis-led Workshop Intensive at Hamilton College, Clinton, NY. June 14-24. Collection of the author (also to be archived at the Grotowski Institute, Wrocław, Poland). All audio recordings have been transcribed, lightly edited and sound quality enhanced under the direction of Diane Edgecomb.

CYNKUTIS, Zbigniew. 2015a. *Acting with Grotowski: Theatre as a Field for Experiencing Life* (Khalid Tyabji trans.; Paul Allain and Khalid Tyabji eds). London and New York: Routledge.

CYNKUTIS, Zbigniew. 2015b. 'Notebook–Diary', in Paul Allain and Grzegorz Ziółkowski (eds), *Voices from Within: Grotowski's Polish Collaborators.* London / Wrocław: Polish Theatre Perspectives / Grotowski Institute, pp. 72–78.

DUNKELBERG, Kermit. 2008. 'Grotowski and North American Theatre: Translation, Transmission, Dissemination.' PhD diss., New York University. http://search.proquest.com/docview/304526932 (last accessed on 16 April 2025).

FINDLAY, Robert. 1987. 'Practice/Theory/Practice/Theory: Excerpts from an Extended Interview/Dialogue with Zbigniew Cynkutis (1938–1987), 26 May 1982, Lawrence, Kansas.' *Journal of Dramatic Theory and Criticism* 1(2) (Spring 1987): 145–50.

Grotowski, Jerzy. 1968. *Towards a Poor Theatre*. New York: Simon and Schuster.

Grotowski Institute, the. 2012a. 'Cynkutis, Zbigniew'. https://grotowski.net/en/encyclopedia/cynkutis-zbigniew (last accessed on 16 April 2025).

Grotowski Institute, the. 2012b. 'Dr. Faustus—fragment'. https://grotowski.net/en/media/video/dr-faustus-fragment (last accessed on 16 April 2025).

Grotowski Institute, the. 2012c. 'Paratheatre'. https://grotowski.net/-en/encyclopedia/paratheatre (last accessed on 16 April 2025).

Grotowski Institute, the. 2012d. 'Theatre of Sources'. https://grotowski.net/en/encyclopedia/theatre-sources (last accessed on 16 April 2025).

Grotowski Institute, the. 2012e. 'The plastiques by Rena Mirecka, Wrocław 1976'. Excerpt from the film *Acting Therapy*. Pierre Rebotier dir., Cinopsis, 1976. https://grotowski.net/en/media/video/plastiques-rena-mirecka-wroclaw-1976 (last accessed on 16 April 2025).

Grotowski Institute, the. 2012f. 'The Tragical History of Dr. Faustus'. https://grotowski.net/en/encyclopedia/tragical-history-dr-faustus (last accessed on 16 April 2025).

Grotowski Institute, the. 2012g. 'Tree of People [*Drzewo Ludzi*]'. https://grotowski.net/en/encyclopedia/tree-people-drzewo-ludzi (last accessed on 16 April 2025).

Karafistan, Rachel. 2003. ' "The Spirits Wouldn't Let Me Be Anything Else": Shamanic Dimensions in Theatre Practice Today.' *New Theatre Quarterly* 19(2) (May 2003): 150–68.

Kumiega, Jennifer. 1985. *The Theatre of Grotowski*. London and New York: Methuen.

Laster, Dominika. 2016. *Grotowski's Bridge Made of Memory: Embodied Memory, Witnessing and Transmission in the Grotowski Work*. London: Seagull Books.

Magnat, Virginie. 2014. *Grotowski, Women, and Contemporary Performance*. New York London: Routledge.

MENNEN, Richard. 2010–23. Personal interviews with the author.

O'NEILL, Eugene.1956. *Long Day's Journey into Night*. New Haven: Yale University Press.

OSIŃSKI, Zbigniew. 1986. *Grotowski and His Laboratory* (Lillian Vallee and Robert Findlay trans and abridged). New York: PAJ Publications.

RICHARDS, Thomas. 1995. *At Work with Grotowski on Physical Actions*. London and New York: Routledge.

RICHARDS, Thomas. 1997. *The Edge-Point of Performance*. Pontedera: Documentation Series of the Workcenter of Jerzy Grotowski.

RUFFINI, Franco. 2009. 'The Empty Room: Studying Jerzy Grotowski's *Towards a Poor Theatre*', in Paul Allain (ed), *Grotowski's Empty Room*. London: Seagull Books, pp. 93–115.

RUSSELL, David. 1983. Unpublished personal notes from workshops taken at Smith College and Hamilton College in 1983.

SLOWIAK, James, and Jairo Cuesta. 2007. *Jerzy Grotowski*. London and New York: Routledge.

WIKIPEDIA. n.d. 'Jerzy Grotowski'. https://en.wikipedia.org/wiki/Jerzy_Grotowski (last accessed on 16 April 2025).

## Praise for *Source Work for Actors*

'This is an in-depth, up-close look at the teaching process and practices of a master acting teacher. It's a visceral, loving account of Cynkutis' radical artistry, his deep dedication to the truth and beauty of the creative process, born in the voice, body, and imagination of the actor. The book captures the "passion and purpose" of this work, and brings to life Cynkutis' gentle, playful voice.'

—**Ellen W. Kaplan**, Professor Emerita of Theatre, Smith College

'Searching for voice resonators in the body, opening to the surrounding environment, especially nature, working with internal images, working with time, working with rhythm—it's fascinating that Cynkutis managed to convey so much to this group of trusted students in such a short time. This certainly places this book next to *Towards a Poor Theater* by Jerzy Grotowski and *At Work with Grotowski on Physical Actions* by Thomas Richards as the most practical and useful compendium for entering the space of Grotowski's legacy.'

—**Waldemar Raźniak**, Professor, Aleksander Zelwerowicz National Academy of Dramatic Art, Warsaw, Poland; Director, Helena Modrzejewska National Stary Theatre, Kraków, Poland

'Diane Edgecomb charts in great detail and with consummate precision what it's like to be an actor in training with Cynkutis. Set in the context of a rural workshop where nature becomes an equal partner in the process, she deftly mixes accounts of working conversations, reflections, her diary entries as well as Cynkutis' instructions, interventions and often revelatory thoughts about theatre practice and his time spent working with Grotowski. It is deeply personal but never awkward, and at its heart are useful and clear accounts of exercises, improvisations, and her rigorous work on Eugene O'Neill's *Long Day's Journey into Night*. This book will inspire and inform in equal measure.'

—**Paul Allain**, Professor of Theatre and Performance, Dean of the Graduate School, University of Kent, Canterbury, UK

'Beautifully written, imbued with depth and sensitivity, this book is an invaluable addition to the literature on the Laboratory Theatre—full of new and unexpected insights on the craft of acting. A thrilling read—essential for the aspiring and experienced actor alike.'

—**Dominika Laster**, Author of *Grotowski's Bridge Made of Memory*